# ALLIES & DEMONS

WORKING WITH SPIRIT FOR POWER AND HEALING

RENEE LAVALLEE MCKENNA, MA, CCH

AWAKEN THE WISDOM OF
YOUR AUTHENTIC SELF

# ALLIES
# &
# DEMONS

**WORKING WITH SPIRIT FOR POWER AND HEALING**

**RENEE LAVALLEE MCKENNA, MA, CCH**

Renee LaVallee McKenna
**Allies & Demons**

*Copyright 2019 © by Renee LaVallee McKenna*

First Printing, 2019

*All rights reserved. No part of this publication may be reproduced, distributed, or transmitted in any form or by any means, including photocopying, recording, or other electronic or mechanical methods, without the prior written permission of the publisher, except in the case of brief quotations embodied in critical reviews and certain other noncommercial uses permitted by copyright law.*

*Book Cover Design by* Diren Yardimli

www.reneemckenna.com

## *Many Thanks*

Early in my life, I thought I had to do everything on my own. I failed miserably. Forced to ask for help, I learned the value of working with others, the humility of knowing my own limitations and the joy of receiving and benefiting from the gifts and talents of my mentors and peers. I tried for years to write a book by myself. Never happened. When I was willing to accept help, it came in abundance.

My deepest thanks to all who helped bring this book into being. I would be nothing without the love and support of my many friends and human allies. Many thanks to John Selby and his lovely wife Birgitta, who birthed the first draft and Chhimed Drolma, who very patiently and gently co-crafted the final version. Thanks to Johanna Maaghul for her sage advice and brilliant referrals, to Mike, Astrud, Dave, Molly, Scott, Rose & Thor, for walking me through my deepest fears and insecurities and for telling me the truth and loving me no matter what. Thanks to Megan for her timely editing advice. Eternal thanks to Isa Gucciardi and Wesley Linam for my own healing journey and for showing me how good therapy is performed, and to my brave clients who share their pain and joy with me and allow me to share their stories here.

*Allies & Demons* provides a powerful process for personal growth and transformation. The journeys in *Allies and Demons* are not a substitute for psychotherapy, medical or psychiatric treatment. These journeys can bring up strong emotions. In undertaking this work, it is your responsibility to determine if you feel stable enough to handle these emotions. Renee LaVallee McKenna, MA CCH, is not liable for any pain or emotional distress that may ensue in the course of this work. It is the responsibility of the person taking the journeys to seek medical or psychiatric help as the need arises.

May I be at peace.

May my heart remain open.

May I awaken to the light
of my own true nature.

May I be healed
and a source of healing
to all others.

1

# Contents

*My Story* ................................................................... 15

**How To Use This Book** ........................................... 21
    *Allies & Demons* ................................................. 22
    *Taking A Shower* ............................................... 22
    *Active Imagination* ............................................ 23
    *Different Senses* ................................................. 24
    *Atheists & Agnostics* ........................................ 25
    *Words Are Powerful* ......................................... 25

## SECTION ONE
# ALLIES

**Our Allies** .............................................................. 31
**Experiencing Spiritual Reality** ............................ 33
    Motivation .......................................................... 34
    Hero's Journey ................................................... 36
    Never Alone ........................................................ 38
    Accessing Power Through Nature ................... 38
    Daniel's First Journey ....................................... 42
    Allies & Demons Workbook .............................. 43

**Calling Power** .................................................................................................. 47
    Three Realms Of Consciousness ....................................................... 48
    Power Animal ................................................................................... 50
    It's Not Shopping ............................................................................. 51
    Honoring Sacred Material ................................................................ 52
    Daemon ........................................................................................... 53
    Calling Power .................................................................................. 53
**Finding The Golden Child** ............................................................................. 57
    All Time Is Present Time .................................................................. 61
    The Gift Of The Golden Child ......................................................... 62
**Working With Ancestors & Angels** ................................................................ 69
    Working With Ancestors .................................................................. 70
    Healing The Grandmothers .............................................................. 72
    Intentions Of The Dead ................................................................... 73
    Teachers In Human Form ................................................................ 74
    Prophets, Saints & Ascended Masters .............................................. 76
    Working With Angels ...................................................................... 77

# SECTION TWO
# DEMONS

**Our Demons** .................................................................................................... 85
**Releasing The Inner Critic** ............................................................................. 87
    The Dark Companion ..................................................................... 91
    Working With The Inner Critic ........................................................ 92
    Lower Power ................................................................................... 93
    Rosie's Story .................................................................................... 94
    Transforming Demons Into Allies .................................................... 97
    Defending Our Pain ........................................................................ 97
    Feeding The Demon ........................................................................ 98
**Healing The Child Within** ............................................................................ 103
    Memory & Triggers ........................................................................ 105

    Seeking Balance & Wholeness.................................................106

    Life Energy ..............................................................................107

    Soul Retrieval..........................................................................108

    Chloe........................................................................................111

    Healthy Self-Parenting ...........................................................112

    Self Parts .................................................................................115

    Gifts & Talents .......................................................................116

    Finding His Voice ..................................................................118

    Emotional Maturity................................................................119

**Transforming Trauma**................................................................. 125

    Integrating The Traumatized Self...........................................126

    Deadly Crash ..........................................................................129

    Denial & Resistance................................................................131

    Jose's Story..............................................................................132

    Return To Wholeness .............................................................133

    Rachel's Story .........................................................................137

**Reclaiming Lost Power** ............................................................... 147

    Rebuilding The Self................................................................148

    Collective Trauma ..................................................................151

    Soul Stealing...........................................................................152

    Power Retrieval Process ..........................................................154

    Codependency & Managing The Life Energy Of Others................157

    Neglect & Abandonment........................................................159

    Wanda's Story.........................................................................161

    Sexual Abuse ..........................................................................163

    Spiritual Harm .......................................................................166

    Spiritual Abuse.......................................................................168

    All Light Casts a Shadow.......................................................169

    Hope........................................................................................171

**Dissolving Depression** ................................................................ 179

    Obligation...............................................................................180

    Fear of Change .......................................................................182

    Conversations With God........................................................183

    Disease Model Of Depression ................................................185

    The Dragon Of Depression ....................................................186

Transforming The Demon .................................................................. 188
Juliet's Story ....................................................................................... 188
Restoration ........................................................................................ 190
Addie's Story ..................................................................................... 191
Suicide Is A Bummer ........................................................................ 193
Shadow Keeper .................................................................................. 193
Liam's Story ....................................................................................... 197
Nourishing Our True Nature ............................................................ 198
Reclaiming Lost Power ..................................................................... 199

**Facing Our Fear** .................................................................................. 209
Faces Of Fear ..................................................................................... 211
Evolving Or Devolving ..................................................................... 212
Procrastination & The Illusion Of Safety ........................................ 212
Doing The Scary Thing ..................................................................... 215
Progress Makes Us Happy ................................................................ 217
The Delusion of Independence ........................................................ 218
Receiving ............................................................................................ 219
Caring For Our Authentic Needs .................................................... 221
Isabel's Anxiety ................................................................................. 221
Make Friends With Our Feelings .................................................... 223
Psychological Torture ....................................................................... 224
Hypervigilance .................................................................................. 225
Epigenetics ......................................................................................... 226
The Twisted Vow ............................................................................... 227
Releasing Fear ................................................................................... 228

**Going Forward: Spiritual Practice In Daily Life** ............................. 239
Daily? Really? .................................................................................... 240
Creating Sacred Space ...................................................................... 241
Journeying In Groups ....................................................................... 242

***Resources*** ............................................................................................ 247
***Suggested Reading List*** ..................................................................... 251

# My Story

*Amazing grace! (how sweet the sound)*
*That sav'd a wretch like me!*
*I once was lost, but now am found,*
*Was blind, but now I see.*

- JOHN NEWTON

In the Fall of 1987 I hit bottom. I hit bottom with drugs, with alcohol, with emotionally unavailable men and with abusing myself with food. It was Halloween and I dressed up in a very provocative Little Bo Peep costume on a Friday night and went to a local nightclub. I carried a staff with a sign that said, "Has anyone seen my f+cking sheep?" I had some attitude and I was going out to party.

I met a man that night who had more cocaine than I've ever seen and I spent the weekend helping him snort it all. We spent some time in an apartment that had no furniture and we had sex on a dirty floor. I stayed in that now filthy costume until Sunday morning, when I went home, changed and borrowed some money from my father. We went to the liquor store and then to the dealer's house to get more coke. On Monday morning I called the job that I had been at for four months and told them that my grandmother had died over the weekend and that I wouldn't be coming to work.

I hung up the phone, opened a beer and did another line of coke. I left the dealer's house that night extremely high, having not slept in three days and with an exciting new plan. I would quit my regular job and this dealer was going to set me up to sell drugs for him at construction sites. He was a contractor. I think he was also a pimp. It seemed like a good career move. I was 23.

That night I went home and looked in the mirror, really looked in the mirror. I didn't recognize the person looking back at me. Her eyes were hollow and hard, her face and body bloated. It is said that you can't scare someone until they scare themselves. I was scared. The gates of hell had opened and I was about to step through. I did something unusual but spontaneous; I said a very brief but honest prayer, "God help me."

The next day I went to that job and gave my two-week notice. Late morning before lunch a woman approached me. She was a forty-something proofreader who seemed kind of grumpy and mostly kept to herself. I'd often seen her sitting at her desk editing. Although we had never spoken, I didn't like her. Her name was Susan Lydon. She's dead now, but she saved my life that day.

She asked me if I got high. I perked up.

"Sure, you gonna get me high?"

She laughed, "No," she said, "only the boss knows this, but I'm in a long-term drug rehab. It's a three-year program and if I leave I go to prison. I want to tell you a story, my story, though I doubt it'll do any good. Everything I touch goes to hell, but it seems like the thing to do. I've been watching you come in late wearing the same clothes you wore the day before, calling in sick a lot on Mondays. I think you might be an addict."

Surprisingly, I was intrigued. We had lunch that day and she told me about her life. She told me about cocaine and heroin addiction, about shoplifting, which was a skill I had acquired. She told me about being a sex worker, selling drugs and her stints in jail.

She also told me about helping start Rolling Stone magazine before her addiction took off, and about writing a book during a period of sobriety. Most of her friends were dead of AIDS. If I was an addict, this is what I had to look forward to. I knew it was true.

The truth really does set us free. I did leave that job, but I kept in touch with Susan. I did not take the "construction" job with the coke dealer. I got into therapy, stopped drinking and using drugs and began a path of personal growth which continues to this day.

Today I understand that I had a spiritual awakening. I've never gone back to my old way of life. Though I sensed it at the time, it becomes more and more clear as the years pass, that my simple little prayer had been answered.

I asked for help and help came in the form of a short, fat, little Jewish woman with glasses and a New York accent. She was exactly the right person at exactly the right time. Coincidence is the agnostic word for grace. I had experienced a grace and I knew it.

I went to a Jungian therapist, which really helped. I was a mental, physical and emotional wreck with no life skills. I test well so I always got A's in school. I was a pretty good artist and I could roll a joint with one hand. Not enough. I started to have panic attacks and it was clear that I had been self-medicating since childhood.

Unmedicated, I needed to do some pretty heavy lifting if I was going to stay sane and sober and have a functional life. One night I saw this man John Bradshaw leading these guided meditations on TV. He called it "Inner Child Work "and it was pretty intense stuff.

Not long after I had an interaction with my mother that left me in rage and despair. This was not unusual, as contact with my mother frequently left me either homicidal or suicidal. The difference was that now I was dedicated to not medicating myself or my feelings.

My Jungian therapist and I had talked about the hero's journey. We discussed the courage it takes to go into the darkness of our own unconscious and face the inner demons who live there. I sat in my car and began to cry for the first time that I could remember. Emotionally I had shut down around the age of five for pure survival and had been at war with my feelings ever since.

My parents prided themselves on being intellectuals and considered emotions the realm of lesser beings. The only feelings that were acceptable in my home were mild happiness or being physically ill. Everything else was called emotionalism, like it was a disease. We had quite a bit of pride about our intellectual superiority, never mind that my mother was a housebound hypochondriac, my father was a compulsive overeater and hoarder, or that their daughter was a bulimic, alcoholic and drug addict.

As I sat in my little Ford Escort on a suburban side street, I began my first descent into the cave to face the dragon of my own feelings. I remembered John Bradshaw's guided meditations bringing people to their wounded child within.

Spontaneously, my active imagination presented me with myself as a five-year-old child. I had locked away this vulnerable part of myself nearly 20 years before. She was in the back of a dark closet, dirty, starving and wearing rags. Her hair was matted and her eyes were wild and sunken. As I approached, she scooted back into the corner like an animal used to being beaten. She was clearly terrified of me.

This is the consequence of how I had treated my emotional self; utter neglect and abuse. I had actively tried to kill this vulnerable inner child because I felt she was the source of my pain. I thought that if I could destroy the part of me that had feelings, then I wouldn't have them.

Not having feelings had seemed like a good idea. That was the goal of most of my addictive behaviors. But seeing this inner child clawing the wall with her dirty fingernails, whimpering in fear, I was overwhelmed with the devastation I had perpetrated on the emotional part of myself.

I told this child part that I wanted to help her now. I promised I wouldn't hurt her anymore and apologized profusely for how poorly I had treated her. She calmed down and listened, but it was clear that she didn't trust me. Why would she?

I invited her out of the closet, but she was too weak to stand. She had been starved nearly to death and I knelt down and lifted her almost weightless skeleton frame and she began to go unconscious.

There was a bathtub nearby filled with warm, scented water. I removed her rags and eased her sore-covered body into the bath and began to comb out her hair. Her whole body was shaking uncontrollably, like someone in shock after an accident. I gently washed her emaciated frame and detangled her hair as best I could. I wrapped her in a thick warm towel and lay her on a stone slab at table height. And she began to die.

I wept deeply and openly in my little car, realizing that I was too late to save my authentic self. Her head rolled to the side as the last breath escaped her bony body. I placed a flower on her chest and dropped to my knees. Grief, guilt and honest regret flowed through me.

Then I became aware of the subtle sound of beautiful singing, and a golden light entered the room. The light began to glow and move toward the girl. It enveloped her in golden radiance and brought the life force back from death.

The girl opened her eyes and as the light shone on and into her, she was nourished and healed. Her sores closed up. Her skin took on a healthy glow and muscle tone returned.

Though she was still too weak to sit up, she looked at me with love and understanding and I knew I was given a second chance at life. I pledged that I would care for her as she had always needed; that I would earn her trust by loving and protecting her in the way I always wished someone had done for me. The light shone on us both and I experienced grace for the second time.

There have been many graces since that day in my Ford Escort.

12 years later I was in graduate school to become a therapist. I had worked as a housekeeper for 10 years in the Boston area and was just starting my cleaning business up again, in my new home of San Francisco. On my first visit to the large home of a new client, she mentioned to me that she was a hypnotherapist. I told her I was in graduate school and asked if we might trade some work, as I was interested in exploring different therapeutic modalities. That was the home of Dr. Isa Gucciardi, founder of Depth Hypnosis and the Foundation of the Sacred Stream. She would be my teacher and personal therapist for the next 14 years.

Upon finishing my work with Dr. Gucciardi, I was introduced to the sister work of Lifespan Integration while on retreat in Santa Fe New Mexico, work I continue to do today.

*Allies & Demons,* DepthHypnosis, Lifespan Integration, Hakomi method, Internal Family Systems and Shamanic journey work all point in a new direction for psychological and spiritual healing which I call spiritual psychology. My hope is that this book will further legitimize the transformative work in the realm of spiritual psychology that I credit with my life and health today.

# How To Use This Book

*Allies & Demons* combines the ancient healing and wisdom traditions of Shamanism and Buddhist philosophy with the best of Western psychology to create a powerful medicine for the mind, body and spirit. Beyond healing our mental and emotional suffering, *Allies & Demons* works on a soul level to empower and activate the authentic self, the source of true joy and fulfillment.

The following chapters introduce the core healing processes or inner journeys of *Allies & Demons* in written form. You may choose to take the inner journeys by following the instructions at the end of each chapter or by listening to the guided audio sessions available at www.reneemckenna.com.

These inner journeys use guided imagery, hypnotherapy and body-based mindfulness to access the active imagination, connect with resources for power and guidance, and heal issues at their core. These grounded tools give form and language to the non-rational feelings, beliefs and internal dynamics that cause our suffering.

Once something has a form, we can work with it directly in powerful ways that improve and transform our relationship with ourselves and others in a positive way. When we resolve the underlying emotional and spiritual problems, our symptoms unravel and dissolve.

## Allies & Demons

This book is divided into two sections of transformative inner journeys. The first section, *Allies,* provides practical resources for accessing spiritual power, wisdom and guidance. These journeys will deepen, improve and enhance your life experience by connecting you in a direct way with the God or Universal Source of your own understanding. The purpose of the entire Allies section of this book is to create a spiritual foundation of power and healing to be able to do the life-changing inner work in the Demons section.

The second section, *Demons,* offers a series of gentle and effective processes that will heal and transform on the deepest levels. Demons are our fears, ignorance, hatred, selfishness, pride and unhealed wounds.

Our demons keep us stuck and cause pain to ourselves and others. They are the destructive habits and forces which limit our ability to evolve and find happiness. Our demons can be transformed and healed. In fact, bringing the light into our own darkness and transforming our inner demons is perhaps our highest purpose as human beings.

## Taking A Shower

The point of this book is to get you to actually do the inner work outlined in the following chapters. Doing the work means taking quiet time to meditate and open your active imagination using the inner journeys at the end of each chapter. Though reading this book may be interesting, reading alone may not provide the deeper change you seek.

Talking about the work of *Allies & Demons* is like talking about taking a shower. We can discuss the warm water, the lathering soap, the smell of shampoo, but rational understanding won't change anything. It's only by getting in the water that we actually get clean.

Knowledge is helpful and important. When the mind understands a concept, it can create a sense of trust that allows us to move forward. That said, it cannot be overstated that intellectual understanding alone is not enough.

Accessing the powerful realms of body, emotion and spirit is essential to become a whole, fully functioning human being. We must connect both our brilliance and our deepest dysfunction in order to heal and grow to our potential, individually and collectively.

We can rationally understand something, but it doesn't necessarily provide the change, relief or healing we seek emotionally, spiritually or physically. Logical understanding is important, even necessary, but the rational mind often cannot access the emotional or spiritual systems where much of our suffering resides.

Taking the inner journeys accompanying this book will grant us direct access to spiritual help and opportunities to heal unresolved emotional issues at their core.

## Active Imagination

In *Allies & Demons* we use our active imagination as a way to work with and conceptualize the non-physical realms. The active imagination is a bridge between our conscious mind and the non-rational realms of body, emotion and spirit. Creating a conscious inner dialogue between our physical, mental and spiritual awareness creates a holistic inner ego-system, where all parts of the self are validated and supported.

Everything we've ever thought, dreamed, imagined, or experienced is recorded in our bodies. Through body-centered mindfulness, guided meditation and inner journeys, we can access realms of higher consciousness, historic experiences and our own emotional/spiritual self.

The active imagination provides concrete forms that allow us to work directly with our unresolved emotional issues and past trauma as well as allowing us to have direct interaction with the spiritual or transpersonal world.

Active imagination can be used to access profound resources for empowerment and personal growth in the form of guides and teachers, ancestors, nature spirits, God/Goddess, or our own highest self. This type of inner work provides infinite opportunities for healing trauma, unwinding dysfunctional systems that underlie many addictions, and repatterning toxic core beliefs like shame, self-hatred, unworthiness or victimization.

Direct access to our emotions, our belief structures, and our stored experience provides a powerful gateway for personal growth. The following chapters offer processes to mend and heal on all levels - physical, mental, emotional, spiritual, energetic, social, sexual, familial, and creative.

Connecting with our own innate wisdom and the creative, healing power of the Life Force is a natural process and surprisingly easy to do. No special training or experience is needed. Access to spiritual, emotional and energetic reality is available to everyone. We simply need to make the time to come present into our bodies, open our inner awareness and receive.

## Different Senses

We're all aware of the basic physical senses of sight, hearing, touch, taste, and smell. However, there are many additional senses that we have access to such as energetic sensitivity, emotional awareness, intuition, instinct, and spiritual insight. Each person has their own unique configuration of how they experience the world, both externally and internally.

Some people are more visual, some are more auditory, some are sensory or intuitive. As we move forward in this work, we will discover our own particular sensory structure.

Don't worry if you aren't particularly visual, there are many other ways of knowing that are just as valid and offer their own unique perspective on an experience. There is no right or wrong, it's purely individual.

As we move forward through the sessions that follow, these alternate or complementary senses will become more obvious and useful both in this work and in regular life.

## Atheists & Agnostics

*Allies & Demons* is NOT a religious practice. Accessing our own spirituality is a very personal, mystical path. A mystic approaches The Universe directly. Trust your own experience first. Everything in this book is intended as a path to your own unique spiritual experience. There is no dogma or paradigm to follow. Every inner journey can be seen as a passage to your own highest self.

If you want to do this work, it's for you to decide. I'm not here to convince anyone about anything. Take what you like and leave the rest.

## Words Are Powerful

Throughout this book I will use a variety of words and phrases to describe and name the Universal Source to which we all belong. The Divine has infinite faces and a thousand, million forms through which we can connect and source power.

Words are powerful and it is important to find language that feels accurate and accessible to us when addressing the Realm of Spirit as a source and resource. Through this work we're building a relationship with the Life Force as we understand it. This relationship is foundational for our health and wellbeing on all levels. Developing a relationship with Higher Power is very personal, so feel free to find wording that works for you and ignore the rest.

Rather than simplifying with one term, I have chosen to intentionally challenge your inner belief structure by referring to The Divine in a wide variety of ways throughout this work. My hope is to expand your understanding and spiritual experience. Please substitute any word or phrase that is most accurate for you when describing God.

After personally suffering years of emotional turmoil, multiple addictions and repeating cycles of anxiety and depression, this work healed and redirected my life. My deepest hope is that it will do the same for you.

# SECTION ONE
# ALLIES

# Our Allies

*Our Soul Allies light the fire in those initial visits,
but it's up to us to keep it burning.*
— S. Kelley Harrell

The word ally is derived from the Latin word *alligare* which means "to bind to." In WWII, The Allies of Great Britain, France, China, the Soviet Union and the United States formed a military alliance to oppose the aggression of Nazi Germany, Italy and Japan. Without the alliance of these many nations, history would likely look quite different than it does today. As nations need allies in time of war, so do we need allies in our daily struggles and challenges.

Most of us have allies we rely on or who have helped us. Our friends, family, therapists, coaches, teachers, neighbors could all be seen as allies. On the material plane, we could hardly survive and thrive without the cooperative assistance of many, even if we consider ourselves radically self-sufficient.

The Allies section of this book is designed to connect us with allies of a different nature - spiritual allies. Spiritual allies are the very real, but unseen forms and forces which can provide the guidance, support and resources most of us desperately need. In modern life, many of our material needs may be cared for, but the state of our souls, hearts and minds are suffering greatly.

In the pages to come and the inner journeys accompanying each chapter, we will connect with a range of spiritual allies who will help us on our life's journey. We will access the power of nature, of a personal power animal, of angels, ancestors, teachers in human form and our own authentic self as the golden child.

We are each a unique expression of Higher Consciousness. We are all part of a great whole. Yet, the infinite power and presence of the Divine, Universal Consciousness, God as we understand God, is beyond our comprehension. We can connect with that power and presence in many beneficial ways and It is constantly making Itself available to us, ushering us toward the fulfillment, joy and wholeness we all deeply seek.

There is so much help available if we know how to access it. Learning to access and integrate the unconditional love, wisdom and power of our spiritual allies is imperative to our evolution. *Allies & Demons* provides a grounded path to connect and work with Spirit for power and healing. Connecting with allies is our first step on that path.

## CHAPTER 1

# Experiencing Spiritual Reality

*The two most important days of our life
are the day we are born and the day we find out why.*
- MARK TWAIN

We are spiritual beings having a human experience. From this perspective, we are never alone. There is a great spiritual reality which is always available to us. It is our true nature and our ultimate home. The purpose of *Allies & Demons* is to empower and connect us on a soul level with this experience in our everyday life.

There are lots of reasons people open to the mystery of inner work, mostly having to do with escaping pain. We might do inner work because we are suffering from anxiety, depression or addiction. We might be coming out of yet another failed relationship, in a health crisis or are just tired of doing the same thing over and over expecting different results. It doesn't matter what brings us here. What matters is that we are here now.

If you want to be free of the past, find hope for the future and live more fully in the now, you've come to the right place. The processes described in this book will change you. They are not a specific road map for success or a how-to manual to fix your life.

*Allies & Demons* is a gate to the unlimited realm of your own highest self and a portal to the unmanifested potential of which we are all a part. The inner journeys offered in this book will heal you, empower you and change you on a soul level.

Living on this soul or spiritual level opens an entirely new way of moving through the world. Doors will appear where there used to be walls, answers will arrive in response to our deepest questions. Wisdom will replace mere knowledge, and a sense of purpose and fulfillment will arise where confusion and fear used to reign.

## Motivation

Pain is a great motivator. It makes us willing to do and try things that we would never be willing to do or try if everything were feeling okay.

Unfortunately, we live in a culture which believes that pain is bad and should be avoided or eradicated at all costs. Certainly, there are times to medicate pain, but there's a risk involved. The risk is that we don't get the information pain offers - that something is wrong, that correction is being called for, that personal growth is required.

There are many ways we medicate our pain. We ease our emotional and existential suffering with prescription drugs, alcohol, addictive relationships, obsession with food, sex, body image, overworking, social media or shopping, to name a few. Even spiritual and religious practice can be used as a way to leave our bodies and deny our reality.

Our roadmap is our own experience. Joy and pain are our compass. Joy pulls us forward to the open road of our own personal growth. Pain lets us know we've hit the guardrail or are driving in the wrong direction. Joy and pain are available as information for us on all levels - physically, mentally, emotionally, spiritually, relationally and professionally. Learning their language and recognizing the gifts our feelings hold is part of the work of becoming an emotional grown up.

Each of us is a unique part of a greater whole. Like cells in a living body, we each have an important part to play in the life cycle and unfolding universe.

On the physical level, we are children of the earth composed of water and minerals. On the emotional level, we are children of our families, culture, race, class and religion. On the spiritual level, we are children of God, aspects of the Creative Life Force that is the ground of being.

Science tells us that our DNA holds the map for our entire body/mind complex. Each cell has a particular job to do; muscle cell, bone cell, nerve ending, taste receptor. In a nearly miraculous way in a developing fetus, cells form, differentiate and find their natural place and function through some deep wisdom and direction we still don't fully understand.

So it is with our consciousness. We each have a part to play in this drama of life. The universe is expanding and evolving and so must we. Resisting this evolutionary pull is the root of much of our suffering. The lung cell doesn't question its role in the body. But human life is complex and many of us feel lost, purposeless and unimportant.

The intention of the journeys in this book is to provide an easily accessible path to the profound wisdom, insight and connections that are our birthright. Each person is a unique creation, a part of a greater whole. Discovering and expressing our authentic self is our most important work in this lifetime. It is the only path to the joy, satisfaction and freedom most of us seek.

Our job as humans is to participate fully in the life process. Like DNA in every cell, direction is available within us if we have the will and knowledge to find and understand it. Deeply feeling our essential connection with the earth and the universe is imperative for inner freedom and fulfillment.

## Hero's Journey

The path of *Allies & Demons* is an updated hero's journey. Joseph Campbell, the scholar and social archaeologist who coined the term hero's journey, found this mythic story in almost every culture on Earth. The hero's journey is an expression of the universal process of personal growth and maturation. Growing on a soul level is our work in this lifetime and the hero's journey is like an instruction manual for how to do it well.

In the traditional hero's journey, there is a terrible demon or dragon ravaging the countryside. The hero goes on a quest to save the village. He challenges his own limitations, slays the dragon and brings back the treasure which the beast has stolen. He returns the treasure to the village for the benefit of everyone and becomes a hero.

Through the work of *Allies & Demons* we learn to become our own hero or heroine. Taken as a map for our own inner experience, each aspect of the hero's journey represents a part of ourselves. The hero is us. The village is our life circumstance. The dragon is our lower self, lurking in the shadows of our own unconscious, messing everything up. The dragon is all the stuff we find unacceptable about ourselves or scary about the world at large.

The dragon steals our treasure by keeping us from our own soul's purpose. It greedily and jealously hoards the gifts and talents of our purest and highest self, deep in the cave of our unconscious. Without this treasure, the village is impoverished or destroyed and we live as frightened, victimized villagers.

Killing or destroying that which frightens or harms us has limitations. If one believes that we are all part of a greater whole, then doing harm to anything or anyone eventually harms us as well. In *Allies*

*& Demons,* our intention is the highest good for everyone involved. This includes the dragon and the ignorant villagers.

From a more Eastern perspective, a dragon can be a challenge in the best sense of the word, maybe even good luck. A challenge is something to rise to, to meet, and to learn from or even be sustained by.

We come to understand the dragon as the part of ourselves we ignore or avoid because it is terrifying - our anxiety, depression, trauma, self-sabotage or that deep wound we've pushed down since childhood. Our inner demons and dragons challenge our safety and security, our sense of ground, and the greatest challenge of all - to our ego-self and the limiting narrative we have about who we really are.

In the traditional Western myths, heroes fight and slay the dragon and become the heroes they were destined to be. In the work of *Allies & Demons*, we need to integrate the knowledge and wisdom gained from the experience rather than running around killing everything we find difficult or challenging. From this perspective, the demon is making a spectacle of itself and destroying everything because, like physical pain, it has a message.

Our inner demons, when engaged and dialogued with, do have a treasure for us - the treasure of how we can face our deepest wounds, fears and challenges to become the hero of our own life. From this more benevolent perspective, the treasure we are questing for is not something we need to rip from the grasp of someone else. It is something we've had inside of us all along - the treasure of our own unique gifts and talents to own and reclaim for ourselves.

Through the power of compassion, the dragon or demon itself is healed and transformed to become a mighty ally, just as intense, but now fighting to support our highest good rather than keeping our treasure buried and imprisoned. Our own hero's journey is that of identifying and liberating the gifts of our authentic self.

## Never Alone

There is so much help available to us if we know how to access it. Whether we understand this Ocean Of Consciousness we live in as our own higher self, God, Nature, or Universal Mind is irrelevant. The truth is that we are part of something greater than ourselves. Accessing Higher Power, The Divine, The Great Mother - whatever your understanding of Source may be, will change the course of your life and your experience of it.

Like the greatest heroes, we do not travel our path alone. We need help. We need to know where to go, what to do and how to do it. The objective of our first journey is to gather spiritual help and discover the sacred inner space where our quest will begin.

The spiritual path we're embarking on is all about exploring and navigating our own internal world. Seeking out important but long-buried parts of ourselves and retrieving the life energy they hold is crucial to our development. The universal call is to heal and transform our inner demons and reveal the magnificent resources of our own highest self.

Because we are all connected as part of a greater whole, what happens to one person, affects us all - positively or negatively. When we do our inner work, we help the village. By retrieving the treasure of our own authentic self, we enrich the lives of everyone we come in contact with, whether we are aware of it or not. From this perspective, any personal growth we do improves the quality of the collective pool of experience from which we all drink.

## Accessing Power Through Nature

The easiest way to access the realm of Spirit for most people is through nature. One of the tragedies of modern life is that we are living in near-total disconnect from wild places and the beauty and power they offer. Historically, we were provided with continual opportunities to engage with Higher Power through nature. Daily life included regular connection with the natural world through farming, hunting, gathering, and walking or traveling with animals.

Unfortunately, in contemporary life, we could spend weeks or even years with our feet never touching the bare earth. Moving from house to sidewalk, into a car or bus, onto more concrete, into another building, and back again.

In *Allies & Demons*, consciousness exists in all things, not only in people, but in places, elements, and all existence. The whole world is a complex configuration of consciousness. We are an intrinsic part of creation; children of The Universe. Sadly, most of us feel disconnected from this great reality. We are like waves in the ocean that don't realize we are actually part of the water itself.

Our first piece of work is to connect with the deep truth that the power of The Divine is always available to us. Using body-centered mindfulness and our active imagination, we access the transpersonal realms of higher consciousness by going to a safe and sacred place in nature. This may be experienced as a beautiful and powerful place that no one can come without our permission. It may be a place we've been before, or it may be someplace new.

In this first guided meditation or inner journey, we will leave the conflict and duality of ordinary reality and open to realms of pure intention that have only our highest good in mind. There are many levels of consciousness available to us. In regular life, or ordinary reality, the intentions of the people, organizations or institutions we engage with are often motivated by their own self-interest rather than what is best for us. Some may even have malintent rooted in their own fear, suffering or desire for power or control.

Accessing higher consciousness connects us with aspects of ultimate reality that recognizes the oneness of all creation and operates from the spiritual principle that the highest good of one is the highest good for all. This is the idea of non-duality, that we are all intimately connected on the deepest levels.

Ordinary reality is frequently based on the duality or seeming separateness that we experience as humans with bodies, minds and emotions often in conflict with others. Duality is experienced as the pairs of opposites prevalent on earth: day and night, man and woman, love and fear, self and other, good and bad, human and Divine.

These tandems of duality work together to create wholeness and point to the oneness which underlies all things. The pull of these pairs or opposites often motivate us to grow and evolve. However, without awareness of the Unifying Force which underlies reality, we experience life through a lens of isolation and conflict. This delusion of separation we experience as humans is the root of our suffering.

The work is to access the spiritual power and wisdom available to us by bringing these higher realms of consciousness into our awareness. Almost all religious ritual and spiritual practice is intended to create this connection between the practical and the metaphysical, to mate the transpersonal with daily life.

In fact, one way to interpret the symbolism of the Christian cross is that the vertical post represents Spirit or Consciousness and the horizontal is the physical plane. Where they meet is humanity. Our suffering is our misunderstanding of this profound communion. Our joy is their conscious interplay.

Most people have had some experience of communing with the beauty and wildness of nature. Even if you have not had this experience directly, it lives in our cellular, ancestral experience. We each have elements that we resonate with. Some people like the ocean, others the forest, desert or meadow. I love the moon. Many of my friends need sunshine to feel balanced. Wind, rock, water and fire are powerful elements that are essential parts of our being. Fire can be understood as our life force; air or wind as our breath. Our bodies are 70% water, with the other 30% being earth elements like carbon and minerals.

The elements are easy entry points which allow us to encounter the Spirit of Nature directly. In Taoism and many other traditions it is believed that everything has a soul, even seemingly inanimate forms like stone, ocean, sun and trees. This non-rational way of gathering wisdom is called *animism*.

In most ancient cultures, the realm of Spirit was a given. Only in modern life, have we degraded the transpersonal to the irrational. Many now worship scientific method and the physical world as the only reality and believe that if it's not observable in a laboratory, it must not be real.

Connecting with Spirit is an experience beyond the intellect. Our goal in this first journey is to discover a place of pure consciousness and positive intention. As aforementioned, the entire first section of this book is dedicated to establishing relationships with power and wisdom which will be resources for the deeper healing and transformative processes in later chapters.

The depth and effectiveness of *Allies & Demons* can be similar to a well-executed surgery. Part of good medicine is to prepare a clean and clear operating room, minimize the opportunity for infection and unnecessary distraction, and optimize the potential for healing.

When we experience a safe and sacred space in non-ordinary reality, we establish a spiritual ground to return to again and again in later work. Simply making a direct connection with the Soul of Nature can be profoundly healing and empowering, because our spiritual disconnect is the source of so much suffering. Like recharging our phone, spiritual connection is vital for us to fully function in the world.

## Daniel's First Journey

Daniel, a handsome forty-something entrepreneur living off the profits from the sale of his second company showed up for his first time in therapy. Asking for help was new for him. He came to me struggling with his relationship with his beautiful, controlling and needy fiance. Seeking a sense of meaning and purpose in his life, he thought starting a family seemed like the next item on the agenda. Daniel had a superior mind. His strong will and self-discipline had brought him worldly success, but he felt a yearning for something more.

When I described this first journey, Daniel looked doubtful. He definitely believed that there was a force for good in the universe, but his analytical mind couldn't grasp the concept of accessing power through active imagination. It was a novel idea that there were non-rational parts of himself which held value.

A lifelong athlete, it was easy for him to drop into his body awareness. Following the simple prompts for the first inner journey, he found himself in a redwood forest. The trees were large. The ground was soft and warm. The light felt almost too bright for him.

I asked if there was anything in this place that he felt drawn to or that seemed drawn to him. There was a circle of giant redwoods. He stood in the circle and touched the largest tree. He was overwhelmed with a feeling of happiness, joy and deep acceptance. He began to weep. Warmth, wisdom and protection emanated from these ancient trees. He experienced a deep trust.

"The bright light is what I feel in the tree," said Daniel. "It's part of the tree. Part of me. Like a total embrace. All I feel is love and this eternal connection. It feels like a family of brothers, supportive and easy. They even have a sense of humor. I'm supposed to surrender to this light. I want to, but I don't know how. The trees tell me to trust myself. Shed all this distraction. Don't be afraid to ask for help and to share."

Daniel had been initiated into the realm of Spirit and now felt that there was something more important than the American dream of a pretty wife and a large bank account. He ultimately ended his relationship and decided to spend the next six months traveling to explore his deeper purpose in the world. Daniel embarked on his own hero's journey.

Not everyone will pick up and travel the world after this first journey, but it may change your life in other ways. This journey is our first step into direct connection with the realm of Spirit. It is our first step home.

## Allies & Demons Workbook

Much of *Allies & Demons* operates in a deeper dimension of consciousness. Inner journey work is similar to dream work. It is common to have a very interesting or powerful dream that's quite vivid upon awakening, but after we have our morning coffee we can't remember what it is. Integrating the information we receive and the power of spiritual experiences into our ordinary lives is the whole purpose of this work.

Writing about our inner journeys provides a link between ordinary and non-ordinary reality, or our spiritual and intellectual selves. After each practice, writing down what occurred will help you remember and also provide a record of your process that may be useful in the future. You may want to get a journal specifically for this purpose or use a notebook you already have.

The *Allies & Demons Workbook* is a companion guide designed to expand and deepen your experience of these inner journeys in exactly this way. This workbook provides journaling questions, space for writing your experiences and prompts for creative expression that may be helpful. You can purchase the *Allies & Demons Workbook* at www.reneemckenna.com.

## *Taking The Inner Journey To A Sacred Place In Nature*

Working with the active imagination is new for many people. We may be used to operating primarily from our intellectual mind and it can take sometime to trust our other ways of knowing. Connecting with Spirit is an experience beyond the intellect. The inner journeys accompanying the Allies section of this book help us establish relationships with power and guidance that will be important resources for the deeper healing and transformative processes in the Demons section.

The spiritual power of nature is always available to us. In this first journey we will use our active imagination to travel to a safe and sacred space in non-ordinary reality.

Many find this inner journey to be profoundly centering and relaxing. Through this session, we establish a spiritual ground to return to again and again in later work. Simply making a direct connection with a peaceful place in nature and the elements in it can be profoundly healing, because our spiritual disconnect is the source of so much suffering.

Take the following journey in a relaxed state, preferably with eyes closed. From this receptive place, we access the energetic, emotional and spiritual experiences that follow and healing begins. You may take these journeys again and again if you like. Take all the time you need. Repeat until you feel comfortable. Go easy but go forward.

*Guided audio is available for this inner journey at www.reneemckenna.com.*

# *Find a comfortable position and close your eyes...*

Take a few deep breaths to relax your body. Let each breath relax you a little more. As you become present in your body, take a moment to open your inner senses of sight, sound, taste, touch and smell. Open your senses of instinct and intuition. This is a different way of knowing and receiving information. Inner awareness is available to all of us. It may already be highly developed in you or you may grow in your trust and awareness of these inner senses as this work progresses.

This is your own active imagination, a bridge between your outer world and your inner world. Don't worry if you aren't particularly visual. You might just sense or feel this encounter in your body or experience it through your other senses. Trust what comes.

Perhaps you can sense, feel or imagine a path or stairway before you that leads to a safe and sacred place in nature, a place that has only your highest good in mind. Notice if the path or stairway goes up or down. Either is fine. What is the path or stairway made of? Is it wood? Metal? Earth? Glass? It may lead to a place you have been before, or it may lead someplace new.

Sense, feel or imagine following this path or stairway now. Just be curious and open. See what comes. We are accessing the spiritual aspect of nature, which is always available to us through our active imagination. We are going to a beautiful place in nature, a place no one can come without your permission.

Follow the path or stairway and step into this natural space. Become aware of the environment. What's around you? Notice the quality of the air and the light. How does it feel to be here? This is a very private and special place just for you.

This is a place of renewal, relaxation and healing. You can do whatever you wish in this place. Feel free to make yourself comfortable. You can rest, explore or move anyplace you like here.

Notice if there is any part of this place, any element or creature here that you feel particularly comfortable with or that seems drawn to you. You might make this connection now in whatever way feels right for you.

How does it feel in your body to be in this place? Feel the air, the sun, the earth, stone, trees or water. You are a child of nature. Your body is 60% water and the rest is made of the same minerals and elements that make all of creation. This is an aspect of your true home.

As you bring your awareness deeper into this safe and sacred place, you might open to the possibility that the spirit of this place is aware of you and perhaps is even glad that you have come. How is it to open to this awareness? How is it to connect with nature in this way?

Take all the time you need here to rest, relax and receive.

When you feel ready, travel back along the path or stairway that brought you here. Bring this connection with nature back with you, remembering everything fully, and open your eyes. This place is always available to you now. Know that we will return here in future journeys.

It may be helpful to write down your experience in a journal or your *Allies & Demons Workbook*.

CHAPTER 2

# Calling Power

*The source and center of all man's creative power
is his power of making images, or the power of imagination.*
— Robert Collier

Seeking a spirit guide in animal form is an ancient Shamanic method for connecting with power and guidance. Shamanism is the traditional practice of working with nature spirits for healing, self-knowledge and spiritual development. Shamanism is still practiced on every continent and in most cultures today in one form or another. From Europe to Siberia and Tibet, from Native America to the Amazon and Africa, our Shamanic heritage offers universal spiritual wisdom common to many indigenous religions and is available to us all.

The essence of Shamanism, found in the Shamanic journey, is both effective and accessible to anyone who wants to explore its potential in their everyday life. This venerable spiritual practice helps us connect with our authentic self, the wisdom of nature, and realms of higher consciousness in a clear and simple way.

This work draws from Core Shamanism, a term coined by Michael Harner of the Foundation of Shamanic Studies. Harner is an anthropologist who traveled the world studying with different shamans. Like Joseph Campbell, he found incredible similarities throughout the world's spiritual healing traditions. Harner distilled the methods found in all Shamanic practice, making this ancient path readily available to the modern seeker.

Shamanic methods present helpful tools for receiving and applying spiritual guidance and information. These methods work in harmony with any worldview or belief system, and help bring us into direct connection with Universal Source however we understand it. Many find that practicing Core Shamanic methods deepen the spiritual or religious foundations they might already have.

## Three Realms Of Consciousness

Conceptual models help us to understand and work with deeper realities. In the Shamanic system there are three realms of consciousness: the upper realm, the middle realm, and the lower realm. In contrast to the Christian model of consciousness, both the lower and the upper realms in Shamanism are considered positive – so we can fully trust that whatever happens in these realms is for our highest good and personal development.

Ordinary reality is where we live now. Ordinary reality is the earth plane, the middle realm, the material world as we experience it in our daily lives. There are many things happening in the middle realm that are deceptive, destructive and harmful. We often can't trust people, situations or institutions we come in contact with. We've all been harmed – and we have all harmed others with our pride, our fear-based words, our selfish behavior. Just like when we're walking down a city street, we have to be careful in the middle realm of life.

In contrast, the upper and lower realms are aspects of *non-ordinary reality*, spaces of clear intention that have only our compassionate evolution in mind. The term *non-ordinary reality* refers to non-physical realms of consciousness like the upper and lower realms. The Shamanic journey provides a path between the middle world and the non-ordinary realms of spirit and psyche. In truth, we are surrounded by Higher Consciousness. In the Shamanic journey we experience this Higher Consciousness by traveling to the upper and lower realms through inner journey work.

Opening to non-ordinary reality matures and expands our capacity to hold power and express our authentic self in the world. Journeying to other levels of consciousness offers tools and possibilities for growth and change not available in ordinary ego-based awareness.

The act of grounding ourselves in non-ordinary reality, in the upper and lower realms, helps us to navigate the challenges of human existence, broadening our awareness and empowering our reserves. It is here on Earth, in the middle realm, that things get wonky. As spiritual beings having a human experience, this is where our work is.

Traditionally a shaman was a spiritual teacher who served as intermediary for average people between the usual middle realms of life, and the more subtle invisible spirit world – similar to the role of priest, minister, imam, lama, or rabbi. It seems that human spiritual development has recently progressed to where having an intermediary is no longer necessary or desirable.

In many cases, intermediaries between a person and the Creator, the Source, whatever you call it, can be a hindrance to our personal development. We are being called as a species to grow. Through the Shamanic journey and other mystical spiritual practice, we encounter The Divine directly. Opening to higher wisdom, clarity and purpose supports human development on all levels.

Personal growth requires change. If you do what you always did, you will get what you always got. Our challenge is to gain the personal courage to move out of our comfort zone. To change, we must be willing to move into the unknown – because that's where new possibility lies.

## Power Animal

In the first guided session, we found a sacred space from which to begin our work. Our next step will be to return to this sacred place to connect with a power animal or spirit guide in animal form.

As we approach this next journey, remember there are many different ways of knowing and communicating with Spirit. We are often limited by being primarily verbal communicators. In everyday relating, we take in a lot of information through body language, facial expression, emotional sharing and energetic exchange. It is helpful to stay open to whatever happens, knowing that what occurs is a teaching for our own development.

Often, like in the dream world, we encounter symbols and forms that have special significance or meaning to us. There are many systems of understanding signs, symbols and archetypes. Both the Internet and libraries are full of explanations of what different symbols may mean. Though symbology can be very interesting, it is recommended not to look to "experts" to explain what particular images in journeys mean.

Whatever comes to us is arriving through our own direct experience with The Universe. It's important to do our own work and determine for ourselves what a specific experience might point to.

Say for example, we have a teacher who is an owl. We can look up what the owl form or image symbolizes. In Africa and the Middle East and among some Native American tribes, the owl is seen as a bringer of death or bad omens. Among most European cultures, the owl is seen as an intelligent being. In ancient Greece the owl was connected with Athena, the goddess of wisdom and war. What we find meaning-wise will depend on where we look. I suggest that you look inside yourself first.

Power animals have much to teach us about our relationship with power, with the world, and with ourselves. The form of the animal, its character, attitudes and behaviors are all teachings in one way or another.

Each creature holds a specific configuration of power, insight and way of being. The particular attributes of each animal have much to offer and teach us about ourselves. In this work, the lion is not greater than the butterfly, the whale not wiser than the crab. Each has something to teach that is unique and distinct.

## It's Not Shopping

Some people think they know what their power animal is before they do this journey because they already consider a particular animal to be strong, beautiful, cuddly or whatever. As one of my teachers used to say, this is not "shopping." The Shamanic journey is a deep and mysterious process beyond the rational mind. Be open-minded and trust your own psyche to call that which will serve you best.

For example, in her second inner journey, Priya discovered her power animal was a snake. She was disappointed. She had hoped for something cooler or sexier like a panther or a dolphin. Priya didn't mind snakes really, but she didn't have much of a relationship with them either. In her journey the snake shed her brown skin and revealed a new skin of beautiful apple green.

Upon reflection, Snake was showing Priya her own relationship with herself. Priya struggled with anorexia, had trouble caring for her body, and often dismissed her own needs and feelings. Her disappointment with her guide having snake form mirrored her disappointment with herself. By shedding its skin, Snake was teaching Priya that change was possible and perhaps already happening for her.

In later journeys Priya came to trust and respect Snake's wisdom and care for her. As she grew in this spiritual relationship, her relationship with herself improved and deepened. Much of the language of the inner journey is metaphor or allegory, pointing to deeper truths we avoid or are unconscious of.

## Honoring Sacred Material

The work of *Allies & Demons* leads to new, interesting and profound experiences. These new ways of understanding and interacting with the inner realms of Spirit can be exciting and even life changing. It is natural to want to share with others. This is our information and we can do with it what we want. However, it's wise to be selective about who we share details with and in what circumstances.

The problem with oversharing is that it can drain the power from the experience and may even have some effect on the spiritual relationships we're building. It's important to honor the work we are doing and be aware of our motives. Inner journeys are mysterious and fascinating, but they are soul level material and should be treated as sacred.

This doesn't mean we should never discuss our inner experience, just that there are appropriate ways to share. Although I talk about this work all the time in a general way, I never discuss the specifics of what happens in my own inner journeys outside of times set aside specifically for that purpose like a workshop, individual counseling session, or when speaking with someone else engaged in *Allies & Demons* work.

The danger in casual oversharing is subtle, but it can tarnish the depth and mystery of the encounter, and tends to be rooted in boosting our own ego rather than growing in integrity and character.

There's an old saying, "Don't throw pearls before swine." This doesn't mean that other people are pigs, but that it's important to share valuable information with people who can honor, hold, and understand its true value. This elevates the process rather than devalues it, and strengthens our relationship with our own authentic self and with the supportive spiritual realms we are accessing.

## Daemon

The idea of having a helpful, guiding ally from the spirit world was known in ancient Greece as a daemon. In Greek thought, each person was born with a daemon. Daemons, benevolent guiding forces that helped define the character and personality of their counterpart, were similar to guardian angels of ancient Judaism and Christianity.

Socrates spoke of his daemon as "a voice which comes to me and always forbids me to do something which I am going to do, but never commands me to do anything." Plato, Aristotle and Marcus Aurelius also spoke openly of their daemons as positive, inspiring forces in their lives.

The word demon was derived from this idea of a daemon in the early 2nd century CE as a form of religious propaganda to discourage connection with the natural world and any form of spiritual help outside of that approved by the church.

## Calling Power

As a general rule, when journeying to a teacher in animal form you'll always enter and exit from the same place. You may travel to different places within the journey, but you always want to travel the same path to and from ordinary reality that was established in the first inner journey from Chapter 1, unless your guide or teacher instructs you otherwise.

Many people find it helpful to write their journey down as soon as they return. After you have finished writing, you may want to take a few minutes to call the energy of your power animal into the room with you in ordinary reality.

In Shamanic terms, connecting with a power animal in ordinary reality is referred to as "calling power." Instructions for calling power in this way are included in the inner journey accompanying this chapter.

Once you've made this connection, it cannot be severed and will continue to inform and transform you on all levels, whether you're aware of it or not. Your power animal is an ally, a primary source and resource for power, guidance, inspiration and assistance. It will be available in the days, weeks, months and even years to come, if you choose to use it.

The inner journey for this chapter is a modified Shamanic practice. In a traditional Shamanic journey, one follows the sound of the drum to get to non-ordinary reality. For simplicity, we will follow the sound of my voice. Holding the intention to go to the lower world to meet our power animal will lead us where we need to go. Both the drum and the human voice can guide us. Each provides a slightly different pathway to the same destination. Like traveling, one can take a bus or ride a mountain bike to get to the same place. Each provides a different experience, but will ultimately land you where you want to go.

If you are interested in experiencing the traditional Shamanic journey, please visit the audio section of my website www.reneemckenna.com for complete instructions including recorded drumming.

# Taking The Inner Journey
# To Your Power Animal

Connecting with nature spirits or a spirit guide in animal form is an ancient practice for healing and empowerment. In this next inner journey we will return to the sacred place in nature we encountered in our first session. Here we will meet our power animal in whatever form is most helpful for us. The form of the animal itself is a teaching. I encourage you to be open and see what comes.

Feel free to repeat this journey as often as you like. Journeying is a spiritual practice and many practitioners find their power animal becomes a trusted resource for wisdom, power and guidance over time.

*The Inner Journey To Your Power Animal is available in guided audio format at www.reneemckenna.com.*

# *Find a comfortable place where you can be undisturbed and take a few deep breaths to relax your body...*

*Take a moment to open your inner senses of sight, touch, sound, instinct and intuition.*

*We are going to set the intention of connecting with a power animal or spirit guide in animal form. No pressure. There is no right or wrong way to do this. Simply hold this phrase in your mind:*

*"I am taking an inner journey to meet my power animal."*

*Now, see if you can locate the path or stairway that you traveled in the first inner journey. When you are ready, follow that path or stairway back to the safe and sacred place in nature.*

*As you step into this beautiful place, notice what's around you. You might repeat the intention, "I am taking an inner journey to meet my power animal." Relax and see what comes.*

*Ask any creature that approaches or you become aware of, "Are you my power animal?" If the answer feels like a yes, stay with this creature and see what they have to teach or communicate with you.*

*If you ask and the answer seems like a no, keep moving. Continue to ask whatever you come upon, "Are you my power animal?" until you get an affirmative answer.*

*When you connect with your power animal or spirit guide, notice what their form is. What do they want to do or communicate with you? What are their attributes and strengths?*

*Is there anything you want to do or communicate with your power animal? Is there anything they want to teach you right now?*

*Stay until this feels complete.*

*When you feel ready, return back along the path or stairway that brought you here, following it all the way back to the place where you began. Gently open your eyes.*

*When you are fully back in your body, take a moment and call your power animal into the room with you now. Notice where you sense, feel or imagine them in relation to you. Are they in front of you, beside you, behind you or above you? How does it feel to have this energy in the room with you?*

*Your power animal is always available to you. Feel free to make this connection anytime. Experiment with calling power in this way. This is a resource we will use in later work and a spiritual practice you can use in daily life if you choose.*

*Write down your experience.*

## CHAPTER 3

# Finding The Golden Child

*Be yourself, everyone else is taken.*
- Oscar Wilde

Our soul's mission is to bring our true self into the world in all its quirky brilliance. In this light, gathering the resources to develop our highest self and follow our joy is central to *Allies & Demons*.
Each person is a unique expression of Universal Consciousness. We all have something special to offer, a contribution to make to those around us. Our work as adults is to discover, support and transmit our own particular gifts and talents into the stream of life.

The golden child is an aspect of ourselves that contains our spiritual essence, our highest hopes and our deepest dreams. It is one of our greatest treasures and natural resources. Generally, this part of our self is full of energy and innocence, hope and creativity, curiosity and compassion. It has a natural sense of connectedness with the universe, and our role in the whole of life.

The soul light we were born with that never goes out is the golden child. In fact, the psyche will do everything it can to ensure the survival and protection of this beloved part of the self.

One of the tragedies of being a human is that most of us lose connection with our pure, innocent, wise golden child early in life. We continue as teenagers and adults with this bright inner source of energy, passion and spontaneity missing from our lives.

Even though we lose this connection, the authentic self of our golden child can never be destroyed. It can only be evicted, exiled or put far away for safekeeping, like Rapunzel in the tower.

For most adults, the authentic self (who we really are) has been forsaken, and a false self has taken its place. Our false self is like a mask that we habitually wear to please others or to get what we think we want.

Many people have no present-moment experience of their true self, or if they do, they reject it as dangerous, unsustainable or fantasy. There can be no genuine fulfillment in life if we don't support, integrate and express our true self.

The golden child within us may be very young. It's a pristine presence deep within that always holds the connection between us and our spiritual core.

At age four or five, a developmental shift happens that distances most of us from our true nature. This is when we start to move out into the world, go to school and develop our individual sense of self in relation to others. Around this age, children begin to understand themselves as separate people who need to function in society. As societal norms are exerted in a more direct way, pressures of family, religion, peer group, teachers, culture and the world at large often force the golden child into hiding or separation in order to survive.

There are many reasons for this separation we experience from our soul light, and the reasons aren't necessarily overtly malicious. It may just be that a mother doesn't like little girls to be loud, or forbids them from playing in the mud. Often a child's natural character and way of being simply doesn't fit into traditional social norms – like a sensitive boy who's expected by the father to be a macho man, or a child with gender variation in a religious community that believes any divergence from their rigid belief structure is a sin.

Unfortunately, for one reason or another, we too often have to disconnect from our authentic self, from our golden child, in order to fit into our contemporary tribe. Abuse or neglect can also drive the golden child deep into hiding. Sometimes our true self shrinks away from our conscious awareness because of emotional starvation, from never being fully recognized, appreciated or supported.

Whatever the cause of our disconnect from our genuine self, the intent of the work in this chapter is to reconnect with this precious part of ourselves. The golden child may have been cast out or buried, but remains alive, pure, powerful, authentic and available to us as adults.

## All Time Is Present Time

For our purposes in these guided sessions, it's key to remember that in the eyes of the psyche, all time is present time. In the realm of inner work, of active imagination, there is no past and no future, there is only the present. As in dreams, everything is experienced as happening in this moment, even memories from the past. When we go to our deepest internal memories, hopes and challenges, we experience them as happening right now.

We can't of course actually go to the past or the future. These are mental constructs designed to help us manage the mystery of life that we call time. We have devised the construct of past-present-future time because our brains need to hold things in a linear way so as to make sense of life. In the ultimate spiritual reality there is only the present moment, emerging over and over into infinity.

This realization of the illusion of time can be overwhelming and make our brains spin in confusion. We conceptualize realities we call the past and the future as distinct from our perpetual sensory location in the present moment. Our deeper sense of time is eternal. It's always here and now whether we are aware of it or not. Eckhart Tolle's book *The Power of Now* is a brilliant, in-depth discussion on the beauty and freedom of this great truth.

In *Allies & Demons*, we go into "the past" and bring the golden child into the present moment to be integrated into our current, adult lives. This is called soul retrieval or inner child work, where we help heal and retrieve parts of ourselves that are stuck in the psychological experiences of the past.

Our goal is to bring these self parts fully into our current lives, so that we may benefit from the life energy and inspiration they hold. In so doing, we will free ourselves from past trauma, neglect, abuse, disappointment and despair, bringing infinite possibilities for hope and healing into present time.

Through the journey work accompanying this chapter, we will use our active imagination to access our past in the present moment. As we start to work with historic child aspects of our self, we find that there is no gap of time separating our memory-experience and now.

Every dream, thought, feeling and experience we've ever had has been recorded in our body, emotions, mind and spirit. In *Allies & Demons*, we use intent, body-centered awareness, and vital help from our inner guides to bring the golden child into our lives.

## The Gift Of The Golden Child

The golden child is a wise and powerful part of ourselves, knowing with full clarity its true identity and power potential. The golden child within is naturally connected with and eager to help manifest whatever gifts and talents we were born with. The life force of this curious, compassionate, creative self can be a source of joy, courage, and wonder when we reconnect with it as adults.

When disconnected from our true nature, we lose access to vital life energy because we're cut off from an essential part of our self. By bringing our golden child into the present moment, we receive healing, power and resources previously unavailable to us.

For example, at the age of five Elena often played out in her garden and spontaneously created ritual spaces using the four directions of East, West, North, South. She would set up elaborate configurations of stones, dolls and flowers in her backyard, naturally creating sacred space in a traditional way. Although she was too young to be trained, and in fact had no teachers available in her community, she enjoyed a very active relationship with nature spirits and with her ancestors, whom she called her imaginary friends.

One day, she innocently picked some flowers in the garden next door for one of her arrangements and her father beat her because the neighbor complained. No one understood what she was doing, and she felt so rejected and humiliated that she never played that way again. In fact as she moved through childhood, she entirely lost connection with this gifted part of herself and with the spirit world.

As an adult, she came to me in deep depression. She learned to reconnect with the elements of nature and how to heal, liberate and retrieve her golden child. In doing this, she also spontaneously returned to the resonance and insight that spiritual ritual and her "second sight" in the spirit world provided her. She found a teacher and began training in her ancestral Yoruba tradition, and then started working as a natural healer helping others in need.

Another client, Jack, a retired policeman, came to me after his wife of 26 years filed for divorce. They had fought for years over Jack's drinking and emotional disconnection from the family. Jack had gone to rehab, gotten sober and joined Alcoholics Anonymous. He was excited about his recovery and felt like the ending of his marriage was a wake-up call.

Jack discovered his golden child during a journey to his power animal. Unexpectedly, Jack was brought to the scene where he had helplessly watched his sister drown in a pond when he was four years old. Ever since, he'd felt guilty because he hadn't been able to save her.

His golden child was frozen and buried away in shame and fear for nearly sixty years. When Jack finally opened to reconnect with this lost part of his true self, he was able to release the grief and guilt he'd carried since childhood. Though he had dedicated his life to protecting others, Jack always felt he wasn't doing enough. He reconnected with the sensitive, innocent, empathic part of himself. A deeply compassionate person, Jack opened emotionally in a way that had been blocked for most of his life. He came to enjoy living alone and his relationship with his children, grandchildren and new friends in recovery blossomed in very fulfilling ways.

For many people, this act of connecting with the golden child in adulthood is our first conscious experience of the authentic self. It opens a window into our long-buried hopes, dreams and possibilities.

Whatever age or stage we might be in our life, whether seventeen or seventy, when we connect with the golden child and become willing to support our authentic self in this new way, life will almost certainly change for the better. When we support our own deeper purpose in the world, we step into the natural flow of life and life rises to meet us in mysterious and wonderful ways.

When we connect with transpersonal aspects of ourselves, positive things will start to happen. Opportunities will come and grace will make itself available the more we live from our authentic self and trust the flow of life. As we experience the serendipity of universal support, the clearer and more available the next right life choice becomes.

In this new session we're going to return to our safe and sacred place to reconnect with our own true nature in the form of the golden child. Each inner journey we make further develops our relationship of trust as we learn to understand and work with the inner power we are gaining access to.

## *Taking the Inner Journey To The Golden Child*

The process we will use to find the golden child is based on the ancient Shamanic practice called soul retrieval. Soul retrieval connects us with our authentic self and returns vital life energy to us physically, mentally, emotionally, spiritually and energetically. Connecting with the golden child is a powerful step on our path to wholeness.

> *This inner journey is available in guided audio format at www.reneemckenna.com.*

## *Make yourself comfortable and take a few deep breaths to come into your body and open your inner senses…*

*Call your power animal into the room, and notice where they are in relation to you. Are they beside you? Behind you? In front of you?*

*Sense, feel or imagine yourself as a young child, perhaps the best part of yourself that's innocent, sensitive, adventurous, compassionate, creative, vulnerable, and most connected with who you really are. The part of you that's available before the cares, worries and experiences of the world covered them up.*

*How old is this child? What is their setting? What is this part of yourself doing as you imagine them? How are they feeling?*

*Imagine yourself as you are today, your best adult self, with all the work you've done and all the experiences you've had. Now imagine yourself stepping into the scene with this child and bringing your power animal with you.*

*We want to tell the child that we are their adult self come to connect with them in present time. Notice how you feel about this child? How does the child feel about you? What's good about this child? What are their gifts, talents, strengths? How have you related with this part of yourself in your life?*

*What does this child have to offer you? How does your power animal feel about them? How does the child feel about this creature?*

*Is the child willing to come to your safe place in nature? If so, bring them there now. The child can do whatever they want in this natural space, explore, rest or play. No one can come here without their permission. Let the child decide what they want to do. How do they feel to be in nature in this way?*

*What does this child need from you? What do you need from this child? Is there anything you need to do or change in your life to be able to love and care for this golden child in the way they've always needed?*

*Does the child want to stay in this place in nature or do they want to come and be with you in your life today? Either is fine and it's up to the child. If the child wants to stay in nature, we want to assure them that they are safe here and that we are aware of them now in a way we've never been before.*

*Ultimately the golden child wants to be integrated back into your own energy system. For now, if the child wants to stay in the sacred place to rest, explore or heal, that's fine. Ask the child if they need anything to feel more comfortable here. Your power animal can help you provide what they need. We will come back and get them later in subsequent work.*

*If the child is willing to come be with you in your life today, imagine hugging them into your body right now. Welcome them home, integrating them into every system of your body, physically, energetically, emotionally, socially, sexually, intellectually, creatively. You now have access to all that is good about this child. You are more whole than you have ever been before.*

*When you're ready, follow the path or stairway you take to this place back into ordinary reality. Once you are back, open your eyes and take a moment to connect with the golden child in present time. Imagine them in the room with you right now and notice where they are. Are they beside you? In front of you? Within you? How do they feel to be here? How is it for you to be connected with your golden child in this way?*

*Write down your experience.*

CHAPTER 4

# Working With Ancestors & Angels

*I believe I am connecting to angels and spirit guides and ancestors.
All of that is falling under the category of God
and that is what I can tap into when I tune in and slow down.*
- Gabrielle Bernstein

Working with non-physical teachers in human form can enlarge our grounded, trusting relationship with The Universe, our true selves and our ancestry. Working with a spiritual guide in human form adds another valuable resource for wisdom, guidance and power to our internal tool box.

The benefit of connecting with Higher Consciousness in these different ways, such as a place in nature, our golden child, or a power animal, is that it gives us different perspectives on ourselves, the world, and on consciousness in general. Opening to these multiple spiritual resources is an expanding, awakening, empowering experience. We are not alone and there is a lot of help available to us when we open to receive it.

Teachers in human form come in many guises and from varied levels of consciousness. Ancestors and loved ones who have passed may provide very personal, emotional, spiritual support. Angels and saints frequently offer benevolent strength while wise beings and ascended masters may grant specific insight, guidance and healing.

Life is a series of relationships with places, things and especially the people around us. One of our goals in *Allies & Demons* is to grow into a mature place of balance and effectiveness. Over time, as we become solid in ourselves, we can be less defended and more open to receive the good life has to offer us, and pursue what matters to us most.

Spiritual development is imperative for our wellbeing and our health. Internal relationships with guides and teachers, with sacred spaces, aspects of God and nature can shift our negative self-defeating patterns quickly and gently. We are gathering strength and resources to heal ourselves. As we gain in personal power and effectiveness, we may choose to help others and the world.

Working with spiritual teachers in non-ordinary reality is a powerful and transformative practice with many paths and variables. In this chapter we will examine some of the forms these teachers might take and make our own connection in the accompanying guided journey.

## Working With Ancestors

Working with ancestors is one of the most ancient ways of accessing Spirit. Ancestor worship and honoring the dead is still actively pursued in one form or another in most cultures around the world.

Ancestral work in *Allies & Demons* is a different way of knowing and looking at our tribe. We are all tribal. Our tribe is the people from which we come. Our tribe is all of the relatives who have gone before us and the communities we feel most nurtured by.

Civilization as we know it started about five hundred generations ago. It is possible to have around one hundred ancestors in each generation. However we do the math, there are literally thousands of ancestors in our tribe.

Ancestor work can be very powerful and grounding, but it can also be painful and challenging. Most people have issues with their immediate family; a difficult sibling, an alcoholic father, a controlling grandmother, a loving uncle who may have died too young. These dynamics exist in all cultures.

Adoptees, African Americans with slave ancestry, and those estranged from their immediate families may feel triggered by this topic. Intellectual knowledge is secondary in *Allies & Demons* - we all have a legion of ancestors behind us whether we know about them or not. Working with teachers in human form can be particularly healing for those who experience ancestral disconnection.

One of the beauties of working in non-ordinary reality is that the past is always available to us in the present. Those who have crossed over may be available, less in their individual personalities than in the principles and intentions they hold for us.

In *Allies & Demons*, working with ancestors extends in both directions. Just as I believe that our personal growth process moves the evolution of our entire species forward, I also believe that it is possible to send our own healing back through our lineage to benefit the ancestral spirits as well.

Space and time are not conditions in which we live, they are modes in which we think. As we explored when working with our golden child in Chapter 3, our conscious mind conceptualizes time as a linear system consisting of past, present and future. However, time is a purely mental construct. In reality and in the psyche, there is only the ever-present now.

In Chapter 3, we brought a child part of ourselves consciously into present time. When gathering the help and support of ancestors, we may also find opportunities to cast our healing in the other direction, back through our tribe, to heal those who lived before us.

## Healing The Grandmothers

Lisa was a frail and bony woman who believed that she was doomed to be abandoned. Her father left when she was a baby and most of her relationships had been with emotionally unavailable men who cheated on her or eventually just left.

Then Lisa met Sammy and at 52 and 56, they fell in love. Sammy was a quiet, gentle man. He was stable, loyal, and crazy about her. As they prepared to marry, Lisa was overcome with a feeling of doom. As we traced this feeling back, it went through every woman in her family line, as far back as we could see. The feeling of doom was passed from mother to daughter in the womb.

"You will never be loved. Your lover will always leave." It was a warning of protection, but also a curse. We called in Lisa's guides and teachers, asking them to be present at the moment that Lisa received this warning curse while she was still in vitro.

Using active imagination, we brought the baby that was Lisa to her sacred place in nature. Lisa told the baby that the message was a lie. The lie presented as a thick black cord made of tar. We gave the lie back - back to the mother, the grandmother, the great-grandmother, the great-great-grandmother, back, back, and back, like pulling a loose yarn and unraveling a sweater.

Then we removed the curse going forward, up through every year of Lisa's life, unwinding and gathering the energy of this lie. We gave this knot of fear and sorrow to her teacher in human form, who burned it in a fire and it became a cup.

The baby received a transmission from her teacher, "You are loved. You will always be loved." This truth filled the cup and she drank the truth.

We ran this new truth though Lisa's life, having many parts of herself drink from the cup of truth, up to present time. Then we sent this truth back through her ancestral line, offering them the cup of truth as well.

"You are loved. You will always be loved." The feeling was palpable in the room. The ancestors were set free, just as Lisa was. She married Sammy years ago and they remain together today.

## Intentions Of The Dead

Working directly with ancestors for spiritual support can be a very nourishing, connected experience. However, the level of wisdom, insight and knowledge available through these family connections may be limited by the development of the ancestors themselves. We cannot transmit something we don't have.

Working with the dead can be an incredibly supportive and helpful practice, but one must be aware that merely leaving the body does not make one enlightened. Just as when they were living, our relatives may have their own agendas. Even though they may have our highest good in mind, they may not have progressed enough in their own spiritual development to provide the guidance we seek. For this reason, it may be beneficial to connect with wise beings of even higher consciousness.

For example, Gabe, a handsome and stylish young man, came to me feeling emotionally challenged in his romantic relationship. He loved his girlfriend, but felt almost physically blocked from committing to a monogamous relationship with her.

We went into the blocked feeling in his body and came upon Gabe as a seven-year-old boy at perhaps the most traumatic experience a child could have. Gabe came home from school and opened the door to his house to find his mother murdered on the floor in front of him. He had no visceral memory of this, but had been told that this is what happened.

His first memory of the scene was sitting on the sidewalk with the police asking him questions. We went deeper into the feeling in his body where he felt blocked and it became clear that the blocking energy came to him the moment he opened the door that day. Through inner journey work, we discovered that the energy blocking him emotionally was the spirit of his dead mother, both wanting to protect him from the tragedy and also in her own death trauma at leaving her only son.

Her emotional intention and connection with him was completely understandable on a spiritual level, but it outlived its purpose and now blocked him from being able to bond in a healthy way with an adult woman.

Gabe seemed comforted by this realization. He left my office that day and I never saw him again. As understandable as this protective relationship was, the dynamic was unhealthy for both Gabe and the spirit of his mother. It kept them both stuck.

Just as different humans have different skills and aptitudes, guides, teachers and spiritual beings possess their own powers, gifts and expertise. Understanding this, we can connect with other teachers and guides for specific purposes as our practice expands and deepens.

## Teachers In Human Form

Most people experience their teacher in human form as a wise, compassionate being who is willing to help them in their life and the personal growth work they want to do. The form these teachers take varies wildly from person to person, but they frequently present in a way that resonates with the needs or life experience of the seeker.

There is a mystery in this work and the forms themselves are part of the teaching.

One example was George, an eleven-year-old boy who suffered from acute anxiety. Children move easily into active imagination and George quickly found his sacred place to be a vast library in a cavernous stone building. George loved to read, in fact reading was his lifeline and his comfort most days.

It was not a great surprise that George's teacher in human form was a librarian with a grey beard and fancy robes. When we would approach the librarian for help, he would select a book from the many shelves and George could read the answer he sought.

Conversely, the idea of connecting with a teacher in human form was a challenge for Dasha. She had a painful relationship with her cold and disapproving mother and her alcoholic father died when she was 17.

A stocky, vibrant woman in her 30's, Dasha had a quick wit and an easy laugh. She moved to the U.S. as a teenager and had a very slight Russian accent. Dasha loved people and the outdoors. She considered herself spiritual, but rejected the orthodox church in which she was raised.

Dasha felt deeply connected to her power animal, a patient, protective baboon, but couldn't imagine a human that would be worthy of her trust. I suggested that we just take the inner journey and see what The Universe would bring to her.

Dasha traveled to her sacred place, a lush hillside overlooking the sea. There she found an aspect of Gaia she came to call Earth Mother, a very fat old woman with giant breasts and ebony skin. Earth Mother's dress absorbed Dasha's tears and her heart received Dasha's pain. The opposite of Dasha's own emotionally absent mother, experiencing the all-encompassing love of Earth Mother healed her abandonment.

Another client, Rod, a welder with strong hands and a deeply lined face, suffered with insomnia since his son was diagnosed with cancer two years ago. His teacher in human form was a fireman on active duty, a compassionate, blue collar working hero with a wise heart and calm, courageous disposition.

Suki was an independent young executive. Her teacher in human form was a traditional Asian martial arts teacher. They met in a dojo in non-ordinary reality. Suki was a fierce feminist and hated the idea that her teacher was a man. Upon contemplation, she realized that her teacher being a man was calling her to open to masculine input in her life, to be willing to take direction and surrender her need for control.

## Prophets, Saints & Ascended Masters

Religious figures such as Christ and Mary, Tara, Buddha, and Mohammed speak to this basic need for human spiritual connection and unconditional love. Relationship with Divinity is central to the human psyche. Many powerful and enlightened teachers provide a direct portal to God through their teachings and life example and are readily available through this practice.

*Allies & Demons* is not a religious practice. However, many who are religious will find easy access to Christian saints, Jewish prophets, Buddhist bodhisattvas, the many Hindu Gods and Goddesses, the Orishas in Santeria and Yoruba, and teachers in any spiritual tradition. Each teacher offers a particular face of The Infinite, an aspect of The Divine that is helpful or accessible to us as individuals. This mystical practice of seeking direct connection and communion with Divinity is powerful and profound.

The Divine Feminine has presented Herself in many forms in my own life. One particularly powerful experience was with Mary Magdalene. I was taking a class on the Bible as literature in graduate school and one day we spent some time meditating on the passage where Jesus reveals himself to Mary Magdalene at the tomb after his crucifixion.

I was raised agnostic and was unprepared for the overwhelming presence of The Divine Feminine through Magdalene. The idea that Christ first chose to reveal himself to Mary and through Mary, was impressed upon me. I felt the special responsibility that women have to bring the mystery of Spirit into our communities.

There was clarity of direction that was particular to that moment. I was told, "Become a Catholic." Shocked, I asked, "Really? You can't be serious." It was the only time I have felt actually "called" by Spirit. The message was that I needed to become Catholic so that I could better serve my community, like learning Spanish if you live in the Mission District of San Francisco.

Within a year I had completed the RCIA (Rites of Christian Initiation of Adults) program and got baptized. I'm a crappy Catholic, but my connection with Mary Magdalene remains a primary source and she is a vital teacher for me and many others.

## Working With Angels

The word angel comes from the Greek word *angelos* meaning messenger. Angels are reported in almost all religious and mythic traditions from ancient Egypt, Greece and Rome through Judaism, Christianity, Islam and Hinduism. In most world religions, they are celestial beings who act as intermediaries between God and humans.

Angels are reported as messengers, guardians and teachers of Divine will. They are often helping spirits at the time of death, as in the Valkyries from Viking mythology.

I have experienced realms of consciousness populated with light beings. Many religious texts report and cross-reference a group of Archangels overseeing the celestial, angelic realm. At some point in our work, many of my clients interact with or are assisted by these light workers.

Generally, angels are energy beings of pure love and compassion easily accessible to humans. In fact, in my experience, the angelic realm is dedicated to elevating the consciousness of all beings.

Each major religious or spiritual tradition offers a particular perspective on spiritual reality. Mystical Christianity has validated working with angels and saints as guides and teachers. Many saints occupy the realm of ancestors, and many ancestors occupy the realm of angels. Whether a particular soul is accessible to ordinary humans depends on their spiritual state at the moment of their death.

In the spiritual disconnect of modern life, many have come to view Spiritual Reality as a realm for the weak and ignorant. Though a huge percentage of our population considers themselves religious or spiritual, when actually faced with the practical reality of working with The Divine, the intellect frequently takes over and the heart shuts down.

The journeys in this work are intended to move us out of our heads and into direct experience of Spirit as It wants to make Itself known to us. Receiving the unconditional love and compassion available through teachers in human or angelic form is a new experience for most people. In previous journeys, we have been gathering spiritual resources to use as an internal home base for strength, guidance, renewal and stability.

This next journey will connect you with a teacher in human form in whatever way is most helpful to you at this moment. I encourage you to be open and see what comes.

# *Taking The Inner Journey To A Teacher In Human Form*

Working with a spiritual guide in human form adds another valuable resource for wisdom, guidance and power to our internal tool box. Teachers in human form may present themselves in different ways. Ancestors and loved ones who have passed may provide very personal, emotional, spiritual support. Angels and saints frequently offer benevolent strength while wise beings and ascended masters may grant specific insight, guidance and healing.

The journeys in this work are intended to move us out of our heads and into direct experience of Spirit as It wants to make Itself known to us. Receiving the unconditional love and compassion available through teachers in human, angelic or ancestral form is a new experience for most people. Through these inner journeys of *Allies & Demons* we gather spiritual resources to use as an internal home base for wisdom and stability.

This next journey will connect you with a teacher in human form in whatever way is most helpful to you at this moment. I encourage you to be open and see what comes.

> *Guided audio for The Inner Journey To A Teacher In Human Form may be found at www.reneemckenna.com.*

## *Take a few deep breaths to relax your body...*

*Get comfortable and open your active imagination. Call your power animal and golden child into the room with you now. Notice where you sense, feel or imagine them in relation to your body.*

*Using your active imagination, perhaps you can feel, sense or visualize a path or stairway that will lead to a teacher in human form. Does the path or stairway lead up or down? Either is fine. What is the path or stairway made out of? Wood? Earth? Stone?*

*Begin to move along this path or stairway until you find some kind of a transition - an opening, doorway, landing, some kind of elemental shift. Move into this place where you'll connect with your teacher in human form. Notice your surroundings. How does it feel to be in this place? This may be a place you've been before, or it may be someplace new.*

*If the place is undefined, foggy or empty, find a way to keep moving in the direction you were traveling, either up or down. We are looking for a clearly defined place in non-ordinary reality. Look for another transition. Once you find a place that is clear and feels safe, notice the environment and what's around you. Follow what feels like the right thing to do. Make yourself more comfortable, rest, move around or explore.*

*Is there is anyone in human form who seems drawn to you or that you come upon or feel drawn toward? Ask them, "Are you my teacher in human form?" This teacher may communicate with you using words, telepathy or with their actions.*

*If the answer is no, keep moving. If you are unsure, you may call in your power animal or golden child and ask their opinion. If the answer is yes, notice how it feels in your body to be near this being. What are their attributes and strengths? What is their character? How do they feel about you? How do you feel about them? How will they help you?*

*Ask if there's anything this spiritual ally wants to do, communicate or teach you right now. Be curious. Observe. Intellectual understanding will come later. Is there anything you want to do or communicate with this being? Take all the time you need.*

*When you are ready, return to the path or stairway that brought you here. Travel back to your body in present time. Remember everything fully and bring this connection with you.*

*Call this teacher in human form into the room with you right now. Notice where they are in relation to you. How does it feel to connect in this way? Open your eyes when you feel ready.*

*Write down your experience in a journal or notebook.*

# SECTION TWO

# DEMONS

# Our Demons

*Sometimes I wrestle with my demons
and sometimes we just snuggle.*

- ANONYMOUS

Our inner demons are the unresolved emotional issues, rage, ignorance and fear that are the root of our pain. Our inner demons are our anxiety, depression, self-judgment, trauma and unhealed wounds. The addictions, compulsions, issues of romance, finance, work and family that cause us suffering can all be seen as demons.

Certainly, there are external demons as well. War, poverty, institutional racism, sexism and prejudice are social demons. In many ancient traditions, destructive storms, floods and other natural disasters were held as demons of nature. Pollution, global warming, environmental destruction and many earth-damaging, unsustainable human practices can be understood as demons as well.

Seeking money, fame, sex or beauty as a source of fulfillment at the expense of wellbeing, healthy relationships or spiritual development, could be demons. Abuse of power, selfishness and greed are demons, too. Even seeking spiritual knowledge or religious experience can be a demon if it becomes a compulsion, a source of pride or a way to avoid the messiness and difficulties of being human.

The purpose of the following chapters is to illuminate and transform these inner demons and our relationships with them. When demons are healed rather than battled or destroyed, we can extract and integrate the wisdom and nourishment held within them. Healing our demons is the alchemy of turning garbage into compost, for the enrichment of our own souls and the lives of those we serve.

## CHAPTER 5

# Releasing The Inner Critic

*It is far better to light a candle than to curse the darkness.*
― William L. Watkinson

Most people have some kind of self-judgment, internal criticism, or even self-hatred that is a constant part of their life. For some, this internal judgment might be a protective voice that keeps them in line. For others, it might be an annoyance that they have to deal with, or something to try and ignore.

Many people live with an internal oppressor that constantly tells them they are not good enough, they're unworthy, unlovable. Some suffer with chronic guilt and shame. Others have a fearful, over-protective inner judge that renders them unable to take healthy risks or be emotionally vulnerable. Tragically, there are also those who suffer with an inner critic so harsh that it can drive them to suicidal despair.

In *Allies & Demons*, it's understood that nothing can live in our psychic space without our permission. Using our active imagination, we can learn to work with our inner critic directly in a safe way, with the help and protection of our personal inner guides and teachers.

In this next block of work, we will explore our internal negativity as if it has a form of its own, like a tenant in our mind/body apartment complex or like a parasite of our life energy. We're going to look and see if our inner critic is a good tenant, or if it's living rent-free and trashing the place. We will then be able to decide if we want to keep the configuration we have, transform it, or perhaps let it go completely.

Sigmund Freud called our inner critic the superego, and held that it was the result of parental punishment-and-reward for behavior. Most children seek the approval of their caregivers. They try to suppress what they get punished for, and they internalize the ideas, beliefs, and behaviors of their family and culture. This internalization serves us as children by enabling us to survive or even thrive while growing up.

Freud believed that the superego is the seat of moral and ethical reasoning, sometimes called the conscience. Usually, beliefs about what's right and wrong are handed down to children without question. Then, the work of becoming a full grown up involves questioning these hand-me-down ideas in order to see if they resonate with our authentic selves. This can be a challenging process, but the rewards are important: emotional balance, mental clarity and spiritual fulfillment.

Life is not one size fits all. We are here to make our own unique contribution to the world, and we can only do this if we are free to speak and act from the truth of our own minds and hearts.

In the psyche, there's always a range of shared experience – and certainly we all have aspects of our self that we don't like. For instance, most of us could use some healing in our relationship with ourselves, especially when it comes to our inner critic's dominance in our lives.

In my experience, the inner critic is often a survival mechanism or protective device that was helpful at some point in life. Unfortunately, once that protective device is established, most people don't realize that they can choose to release it and be free from conditioned self-criticism.

As adults, part of good self-care is keeping our house in order, arranging our living space so that it's organized and enjoyable. It's important to get rid of broken appliances, thread-bare furniture, and clothing that doesn't fit. The same is true for our psyche. For instance, rather than tolerating the inner critic like a mean aunt who lives upstairs that we feel obligated to take care of, we can actually ask her to move out.

It's important to understand our relationship with our inner critic, and why we've allowed it in our life in the first place. Then we can decide if this inner critic actually serves us today. If not, we can transform that mental function, or choose to release it completely.

People very often ask if it's really possible to let go of something that's been with them for years or even decades. The answer is a resounding yes. The process of letting go can be life-changing.

I've worked with many people who have lived in tremendous inner turmoil with a relentless punisher in their head. After moving through the letting go process called Transforming Demons Into Allies, they have become completely and permanently free of inner torment. I've been through this experience myself, with lasting positive results.

My own internal self-criticism was such that no matter how well my day was going, no matter what I'd accomplished, there was always a knock-down voice to remind me of all the things I had done wrong in my life. This inner critic told me how fat my thighs were, how loud my voice was – and reminded me of all the little things I did imperfectly every day. I was never good enough. Nothing was ever acceptable to that voice inside me. God forbid I ever made a genuine human mistake. This ongoing tirade of self-abuse literally drove me to drink to drown it out and gain at least temporary relief.

If anybody had ever talked to me the way the critical voice in my head talked to me, I would have punched them in the mouth. I'm deeply grateful to report that release from self-criticism is at hand. I've personally been free of that voice for over 25 years, and it's never come back. Dissolving the inner critic uncovered other layers of how I felt about myself, layers that also needed work. That critical, self-hating voice can definitely be released, or transformed into something more constructive.

Self-abuse is still abuse. It is no better to harm oneself than it is to harm others. We ourselves are human beings just like everyone else. We deserve to be freed from the source of self-abuse, which is our own judgment, self-criticism and self-hatred.

Note that logically, if there's a critic, there's a part of us that's being criticized. If there's self-hatred, there's a part of us that's being hated. If there's judgment, there's often a part of the self that's being judged. Too frequently, who we're abusing with our critical mind is our inner child, whether we are aware of it or not. So, in reality, we're talking about child abuse.

The first step in putting an end to inner child abuse is to shine light on what's chronically happening inside us, bringing our conscious awareness to see the situation. Most of us are quite busy defending ourselves by avoiding or medicating that internal critic.

In my experience, we're still responsible. There's always some level at which we have agreed to this internal abuse dynamic, whether we know it or not. It's important to understand how and why we developed this critic in the first place, so that the situation doesn't repeat itself.

The first step is to notice how we experience our own internal negativity. When we open this up, there may be many layers to it. It's not unusual to find more than one critic inside us. We will want to deal with the most presenting, the loudest, the most difficult one first. We'll need to locate the weed, and then pull the weed up by its roots so that it doesn't grow back. To find the roots, first we clearly identify the weed.

## The Dark Companion

Jim, a computer programmer in his early fifties, had been suicidal most of his life. He was plagued with insomnia and had to sleep with the television on to drown out the voices in his head. Over time we worked through the many layers of inner turmoil and Jim became free in a way he never thought possible. The first inner critic we worked with was by far the most nasty and dangerous.

The energy of Jim's inner critic lived in the back of his head and neck, like a dark, cold entity standing behind him. When we followed the path of the terrible voice he had inside which told him that he was no good and should just die, we ended up in a memory of Jim as a toddler in foster care. Jim lived in foster care for 18 months before his adoptive family found him.

Because he was given up by his parents, he came to believe he was fundamentally bad. Children have a very limited world view. They make sense of their experience as being related to themselves.

When a fetus lives in their mother's womb for nine months, they become attuned to the sounds of the mother's body, her emotions, her spirit and her energy. Although they don't have words to describe this, newborns are completely aware of losing connection with their mother. This is a body-felt experience, which is very hard to address through traditional talk therapy.

Jim's pre-verbal belief that he was bad permeated his existence. His inner critic provided a narrative that explained his emotional experience and eventually evolved into the ominous voice that told him he was worthless and should die. Although it was destructive and debilitating, he had a surprising attachment to it.

Tragically, this inner demon, who he came to call The Dark One, was also a companion for him, like an abusive friend who promised never to leave him so he wouldn't have to be alone.

Jim struggled with spiritual connection. In fact, this inner voice interrupted more than one attempt at connecting with a spiritual ally. After one discouraging session, I felt a very strong positive presence enter the room. I asked Jim to drop into his body and see if he felt something at his feet. This big burly man burst into tears.

"It's Lucky," he said. "My dog. She died when I was 12. She's the only thing I believed really loved me in my life." So we began to work with the spirit of Lucky and the little boy who was left in foster care.

As The Dark One dissolved during the Transforming Your Demons Into Allies process, Jim expressed his gratitude to it and wished it well. The dark energy was replaced by a grounded compassionate oak tree with deep roots and spreading branches which loved and supported Jim's inner child.

Although there were many other issues to work through, Jim reported that the suicidal thoughts which plagued him since childhood never returned. Jim deepened his relationship with his adoptive family and eventually hired a private investigator to find his birth family which was a very healing experience for him.

## Working With The Inner Critic

People experience the inner critic lots of different ways. It may be a voice that seems to speak in your head. It might be the voice of your mother or your grandfather or teacher. It may sound like your own voice, or it may be something unto itself.

The inner critic may also be a sensory experience, like mental fogginess or a confusion that comes and goes. It may be an emotional felt-experience, like guilt, anxiety or shame, rather than words. Sometimes the critic is hungry for a certain type of food, alcohol, drugs or a particular type of sex that you feel guilty or shameful about later. Everybody experiences the inner critic in their own way.

Usually our inner negativity is rooted in fear, centered around avoidance tactics to dodge pain and rejection. It's also important to observe that internalized negativity tends to be dishonest. It's not uncommon to have an internalized abusive relationship where the inner critic will say that it's helpful to you, that you can't live without it. In reality, the inner critic is feeding on your fear, your sadness, or on your life energy.

The inner critic may truthfully have been helpful when you were 6 or 10. The question is - is it really helpful today or just fooling you, taking advantage of you so that it can continue feeding and sustaining its own unnecessary presence at your expense?

## Lower Power

Many of us have learned to move ourselves forward using the inner critic as our taskmaster. Internalized shame, blame, harassment, humiliation, fear, hatred or abuse are powerful motivators. These destructive dynamics can become habit. I call this *lower power*.

Lower power is definitely power, in that it fuels us to action, but it is generally destructive. Typically, lower power is harmful on some level, spreads difficult feelings and is rooted in fear. Higher power on the other hand is constructive, encourages personal growth of self and others and spreads goodwill.

Usually we turn to lower power in desperation, when we believe we don't have access to higher power (like love, joy, hope, trust, creativity, courage, honesty or connection) and settle for whatever we can get.

Sometimes our relationship with the inner critic becomes the only way we know to motivate ourselves and informs the way we relate with others. Lower power can become our primary operating principle.

The inner critic turned outward becomes judgment, criticism, control, revenge, resentment, rage, jealousy, shame, humiliation, martyrdom, greed and abuse. These attitudes and behaviors produce strong emotions. These fear-based emotions are the fuel of lower power.

Fear is a powerful motivator and it can be a source of energy in that it can move us forward. But making decisions based on fear and lower power robs us of the inner peace most of us crave.

There are many ways we use lower power. Gossip is a common lower power. It feeds our own sense of superiority at the expense of others. Anger has its place to protect us from harm or injustice, but anger can also be used to create fear and violence.

One might steal power from others by harming them physically, emotionally, sexually, mentally or spiritually. Or someone might gain lower power by abandoning themselves and collapsing, manipulating, or forcing others to take care of them – or even by losing the will to live. We can understand terrorism, war, racism and most social suffering as rooted in lower power.

Our work is to become aware of how we source power, to release our attachments to lower power and grow in our willingness to use constructive motivations to guide us.

## Rosie's Story

Frequently, the inner critic is a protective device designed to keep us safe from rejection, hurt, vulnerability, humiliation, disapproval or abandonment. Unfortunately, too often the inner critic creates internally the very experience that it was designed to help us avoid.

An extremely overweight mother of three with a stressful position as HR Director for a large corporation, Rosie was smart, funny and successful in worldly terms, but deeply unhappy internally.

"I have everything a woman could want," she reported. "A nice house, good job, kids, a kind husband. What's wrong with me? I can't stop gaining weight and I hate myself for it."

Rosie had gained and lost literally hundreds of pounds over the years, but could never maintain a comfortable weight. When we uncovered her inner critic, we encountered a vile, reptilian entity with an insatiable appetite.

The intent of this aspect of herself was to keep her from overeating, but paradoxically it ended up creating the same dynamic it was trying to stop. Every time Rosie was hungry, the inner critic would admonish her to not eat. It told her she was weak, stupid, fat and worthless.

The inner narrative was that she should be better than she was. It deemed her a failure because she had so many advantages and such a perfect life. She should be ashamed for feeling needy at all. Feelings of hopelessness, isolation and despair would ensue and Rosie would be compelled to eat just to silence the inner voice.

When she was stuffing food into her mouth she went into a kind of trance, often in front of what she called "mindless TV." Although the relief was temporary, it seemed better than no relief at all. But then, after eating in this way, she would feel even worse.

Rosie was caught in a vicious cycle of trying not to eat, being victimized by her own self-hatred, using food to numb the inner turmoil, and then trying not to eat again, over and over. The inner critic was actually creating and perpetuating the very cycle it was supposed to be preventing.

In *Allies & Demons* we always seek the deepest need driving an issue. When we can heal the root, the dynamic will unravel or resolve itself naturally.

Using the Transforming Demons Into Allies process, which we will explain later in this chapter, we found the underlying need of the critic and of Rosie herself, was to be loved. Although she reported that her husband was nice, they had a sexless, surface relationship which was unfulfilling for her. Rosie felt emotionally and physically deprived and unloved. At the same time, she felt guilty because her material life seemed enviable.

By feeding Rosie's inner critic the love it craved to its complete satisfaction, the hateful reptile dissolved and was replaced by Juno, the Roman goddess of love and marriage. Juno was a powerful feminine force, offering unwavering strength, support and unconditional love to Rosie.

When we explored the circumstances that created this inner critic, we found Rosie as a seven-year-old girl feeling lonely and misunderstood. She recalled beginning to eat emotionally right around that age.

Using the soul retrieval process that we will explore in the next chapter, we were able to reconnect Rosie with her own authentic needs in a direct way through this wounded child part of herself. As she came to honor and address her own deep needs for authentic love and connection, she was able to name the deprivation she felt in her marriage. Her husband genuinely loved her, was dedicated to their relationship and they entered couples counseling together.

Rosie continues to work with her perfectionism and food issues, but from a place of love and compassion rather than one of self-abuse. Her pattern of compulsive eating is much less frequent and Rosie now practices connecting with her underlying emotional and spiritual needs when the cravings come, rather than just being overtaken by them.

## Transforming Demons Into Allies

We all have an inner critic. In Western psychology, this process of self-judgment is regarded as a necessary aspect of the ego. In *Allies & Demons*, our inner judgment and self-hatred are approached differently. They ultimately dissolve altogether or become transformed into a more helpful or supportive formation using a practice called Transforming Demons Into Allies.

Transforming Demons Into Allies is inspired by the Feeding Your Demons process developed by Lama Tsultrim Allione, a modern Buddhist teacher and founder of Tara Mandala, a spiritual center in Colorado. This method is based on the work of 11th Century female yogini, Machig Labdron and is particular in approaching inner negativity with generosity and compassion rather than fighting or attempting to destroy it. When we follow the Transforming Demons Into Allies process found at reneemckenna.com, we can heal our patterned suffering, achieve freedom and inner peace.

In the journey accompanying this chapter, we will transform hatred, fear and ignorance into an asset for expanding wisdom, power, and love.

## Defending Our Pain

Demons can be understood as our misguided responses to challenging life experiences. We each have unique ways to defend and deflect our pain and weakness. Truly there are infinite variations of self-defense. Our defensive structures often develop as children to protect us from pain, rejection, humiliation or abuse. These defenses are survival skills and may even save us at a particular time in our lives. As we grow and mature they outlive their usefulness. Because we never consciously let them go, they crystallize and become habit. Eventually, these defenses or inner demons become a working part of the self. The defenses that were helpful at one point can take on a life of their own, like a house guest who never leaves or a wound that becomes an abscess.

Over time these defenses can become debilitating, self-perpetuating demons rooted in fear and pain. They become destructive patterns that strangely come to feed on the very energy they came to protect against.

Under every defense is a wound. The cause of the wound is an unmet need. When the authentic need is met, the defense dissolves or transforms. This is the gift of healing our demons.

## Feeding The Demon

Alicia, an attractive forty-year-old with sparkling blue eyes, desperately wanted to have a baby, but could not maintain a romantic relationship. In fact, even having close friends was a challenge for her. Intimate connection was simply too frightening and uncomfortable and Alicia either ended relationships within a few months or chose men who were non-committal.

As a child, her mother suffered from Bipolar Disorder and had uncontrollable bouts of screaming rage alternating with suicidal depression. Although she was rarely physically violent, her mother's verbal tirades were traumatic for Alicia as a sensitive child. Alicia retreated into her world of books, which ultimately served her well in her professional work as a researcher.

Alicia wanted to work on her fear of intimacy. When we clarified the body sensation of fear and aversion, it presented as a black and silver fog that was choking her. It had cold eyes and fed on her fear.

The fog was a metaphor for her inner survival mechanisms. Fog protected her from being vulnerable or trusting others. The fog believed that opening to people was unsafe and getting close was dangerous.

Because Alicia's mother had been so unpredictable, Alicia had shut down as a way to survive the emotional turmoil of her home. Unfortunately, as she grew older, Alicia carried this attitude of distrust with her into every relationship and unconsciously acted as if all people were as unpredictable and volatile as her mother.

Through Transforming Demons Into Allies, we offered a honey-like nectar to this fog with the quality of peace and safety that Alicia most needed. As the fog absorbed the honey it turned into a white moth that was equally comfortable in the darkness and the light. It was delicate, but trustworthy and full of the will and wisdom to survive.

Not long after our work, Alicia had her eggs harvested and fertilized and decided to birth a baby on her own.

## *Taking The Inner Journey To Transform Demons Into Allies*

The focus of this particular inner journey is to dissolve our inner demons of fear, self-judgment and self-hatred using the Transforming Demons Into Allies process. Please note that this journey can be used to transform any inner conflict, unresolved emotional issue or unhealthy pattern we might have.

In this process we dissolve, transform or heal the inner critic or whatever personal demon we are focusing on, using the energy of compassion. By discovering the core need underlying the inner critic, we find the antidote to the unresolved emotional suffering driving this destructive dynamic. We can then feed the inner critic the love, safety, connection, value, wholeness or compassion it most deeply needs.

When our deepest needs are filled, our defensive structures become unnecessary and we can open to higher power and healthier, more constructive ways of living.

This inner journey may be done repeatedly as we integrate and heal our wounds and grow in emotional vulnerability and maturity. The more we make peace within ourselves, the greater peace we will have in the world around us.

*This inner journey is available in guided audio format at www.reneemckenna.com.*

# *Take a moment to become present...*

*Notice how you experience the inner critic. Is it a voice? A body sensation? A feeling?*

*Where does the inner critic live in your body? Does it have a color? A shape? A density? A temperature?*

*Imagine moving this energy of the inner critic out of your body and personifying it with limbs, a head and face. What size is it? Does it have a gender? What's it's emotional state or character?*

*What does this demon want? What is its purpose? What does it feed on or get out of being with you? What does the demon really need? What is it's deepest most vulnerable need?*

*Imagine that your body dissolves into a nectar or elixir that is exactly the qualities that the demon most deeply needs. What is the quality of the nectar?*

*The nectar moves towards the demon and it can take it in, drink it, receive what it most deeply needs. The nectar might absorb through the covering of its body, pour over it or into it. How does the demon receive what it really needs?*

*There is an unlimited supply of nectar. The demon can drink, absorb or receive to it's complete satisfaction. Take all the time it needs to receive. Observe what happens. Does the demon change how it looks or feels? Does it dissolve?*

*Once the demon is completely satisfied, ask if it is an ally in this transformed state or if it needs to move on to the next place for its own evolution. If it needs to move on, the nectar can transport it away, or your guides can escort it safely to the next place.*

*If the demon is now an ally, we will ask it the following questions. If the demon moved on, then ask for an ally to appear. Be open to what comes.*

*What is the form of the ally that appears? What are the ally's strengths? How will this ally help you? How will it protect you? What* vow or promise does the ally make to you? How can you connect with this ally?

Imagine that the energy of the ally pours into your body. Notice how this energy is transmitted, where it enters your body. What are the qualities of this energy?

Once you are filled with the energy of the ally, bring your awareness back into the room and open your eyes. Take a moment and call the ally into ordinary reality. Notice where the ally is in relation to you. How does it feel to have them here?

Write down your experience.

## CHAPTER 6

# Healing The Child Within

*If you bring forth what is within you,
what you bring forth will save you.
If you do not bring forth what is within you,
what you do not bring forth will destroy you.*
- GOSPEL OF THOMAS, GNOSTIC GOSPELS

No one survives childhood unscathed. We incarnate to evolve and grow, so everyone who puts skin on and walks on two legs has issues, otherwise we wouldn't be in human form. I've never met anyone who had a perfect childhood. Things will happen. Caregivers are imperfect. Our needs don't get met. We all have difficult experiences in life. It's how we deal with or process our challenges that determines the course of our lives.

How do we manage the abuse or neglect we experience? How do we deal with our discomfort, powerlessness and not getting what we want or need? Children don't have much power. They can't go out and fend for themselves. They are at the mercy of the adults responsible for them.

In inner child work, we are looking at how our psyche managed our experience in early life. Some people may be lucky enough to just have one or two wounded self parts. Most people have many inner children to heal, care for and integrate. For many, like myself, this is a lifetime practice.

Each time we make peace with a lost part of ourselves, we become more whole and complete. We grow in our capacity to hold our own power and to manifest this power in service of others and the world.

In bringing loving kindness to our lost inner child parts, we also grow in the ability to parent ourselves with presence and compassion. When our internal landscape is grounded in self-care, we create for ourselves the environment of emotional and mental nourishment we have always craved.

When working with our inner child, it's as if this child is an actual individual with unique experiences that we might not have access to with ordinary awareness. In fact, we may have consciously or unconsciously blocked childhood experiences in an attempt to avoid or manage pain and trauma we couldn't process or handle at the time. Some may block specific painful or difficult memories. Others may have no memory of entire sections of their early life. A few may have no memories at all before the age of twelve or fourteen.

When we lose authentic parts of ourselves in this way, a void is created in the psyche. This void is often a place where inner self-criticism and destructive, defensive patterns can come in to fill the gap. Though the inner negativity may serve to keep our authentic suffering at bay, as we looked at in Chapter 5, the suffering created by our defenses may be exponentially greater than the original suffering we hoped to avoid.

## Memory & Triggers

Memory is a constructive mental process. Blocked memories are a safeguard by the psyche, a particular way to manage suffering. Much like putting smelly garbage in the garage so that it doesn't stink up the house, the psyche has the capacity to bury painful memories outside of consciousness. This is a brilliant management technique that allows the self to function when it doesn't know how to process reality.

In *Allies & Demons*, inner child parts are actually fragments of our own soul trapped in psychological time. The fragments in cold storage are disconnected from the whole. Still, they have tremendous impact on our daily lives because they are a part of us, even if we are unaware of them. Usually they remain frozen in the place, time or experience that we hoped to evade.

Unfortunately, this configuration keeps a part of us perpetually stuck in a state of fear, pain or trauma and creates soul loss by keeping a part of our life energy out of reach.

The causes of soul loss, or inner self-division are many. It might be a single traumatic event, or the internal splitting might be the result of some chronic, ongoing dynamic in our childhood like abuse, neglect, rejection or feeling misunderstood.

This internal separation is why certain situations can trigger powerful childlike emotional, mental and even physical responses in adulthood. A trigger is when an experience or thought in present time causes a reaction, like pulling the trigger of a gun causes a bullet to shoot. Emotional triggers can feel quite violent and often show up unexpectedly and inconveniently. A trigger, or strong reaction, is a clue that there is unresolved emotional material.

For example, Max was having sex with his new girlfriend, Josephine. Josephine was a nice young woman and they really liked each other. In the middle of making love, Max was overcome with anxiety and lost his erection. Josephine was surprised at the sudden change and asked what was wrong. Max could barely speak he was so upset, but he was also embarrassed and shocked himself. He didn't really understand what happened either. He assured her that she hadn't done anything wrong.

Max started having nightmares or what is often called flashbacks of being sexually abused by his priest as a boy. He felt a lot of shame and blocked the memory as best he could. However, the actual rape experience was stored in his body. He had sex many times since the abuse, but something about the experience with Josephine triggered the past trauma.

Using inner child techniques and power retrieval, which we will discuss later, Max was able to process what happened and shift his relationship with himself, his past experience and his sexuality.

## Seeking Balance & Wholeness

The higher self is always seeking balance, healing and wholeness. Inner child fragments can be exiled, abandoned and neglected, but they cannot be destroyed and are forever trying to return home. Phobias, addictions, compulsions, depression and anxiety are often rooted in an attempt to keep these unwanted memories and feelings at bay.

Memories, like thoughts in general, are patterns of neurons firing in our brain. Feelings and emotions are stored in our body in a similar way. Working with the sensations and feelings in the body is known as somatic psychology. As we shall see in many of our inner journeys, working with sensations in the body is a very direct way to process stored and unresolved past experience.

In *Allies & Demons* we heal and integrate our past in an empowering way. We do not re-experience our past painful experiences. We already lived through them once. In fact, one of the hallmarks of unresolved emotional issues is re-feeling or re-experiencing the pain or fear of the original unresolved event over and over, either by being triggered in present time or by being drawn to similar situations.

The challenge is that memories with similar patterns can be activated at the same time. Grief, trauma and abandonment memories are stored in a similar way. So when we experience a loss in present time, other unresolved feelings may be brought up as well.

The good news is that these patterns can be reconfigured. Our body/mind system is incredibly plastic and malleable. The possibility for constructive change is ever present. Unresolved feelings being triggered presents an opportunity to heal. From the perspective of *Allies & Demons*, our repetitive negative patterns in relationship and life experience are attempts by these soul parts to create opportunities to evolve and re-integrate.

The purpose of inner child work is to retrieve the life energy attached to unresolved emotional material. We process and digest the experiences of our past, integrate whatever can nourish or inform us and let go of what no longer serves us. Like a cucumber transforming into a pickle, the process cannot be reversed.

## Life Energy

In this work, we act as our own first responders, rescuing the inner child with the help of our own adult self, our guides and teachers. We bring the child out of the situation that has been frozen in the psyche and into the safe and sacred place in nature found in the first journey.

All inner child parts hold vital life energy as well as specific gifts and talents usually associated with our authentic self. The life energy of the inner child is part of our own soul substance.

When we lose access to our child self, we also lose access to the creativity, curiosity or compassion they hold. We may lose the capacity to love and be brave or trusting. We may lose excitement and enthusiasm for life or whatever other wonderful gifts the child has. When we cut off parts of our experience, we defend against historic pain, but we also lose all the things that are valuable about that part of ourselves. Tragically, when we separate from aspects of ourselves to avoid pain, we also lose access to their light.

When we disconnect from our true self in this way, it's like an eight cylinder car that's firing on only five cylinders – we lose power and function poorly. Through the inner journey accompanying this chapter, we bring our wounded child parts home through a process called soul retrieval. Soul retrieval returns and reintegrates lost or separated parts of the self to their natural place. The metaphorical engine of our mental/emotional/spiritual/physical selves is restored to full power. When all of our cylinders are firing, life runs more smoothly in every area.

Inner child work offers a powerful gift - regaining access to the soul energy and the unique characteristics that are often the best parts of us. Our objective is to have a healthy internal relationship with our inner child part in waking consciousness. Some people understand this as an emotional part of themselves. Some would call it their unconscious. Others understand inner child parts as a spiritual or soul component. The ultimate goal is for the child self to become a thriving part of us, living with us in our ordinary life, receiving the love and care they have always needed.

How we relate internally with ourselves is central to our whole experience of the external world. Whether we are aware of it or not, we may have abandonded essential parts of ourselves. Although abandonment may not have been the original plan, fundamentally that's what can happen.

## Soul Retrieval

What happens if we don't do this work? We have an area of our psyche that isn't functioning as an adult. There will be areas of our life where we remain childlike, immature and underdeveloped. We will respond or react from this wounded child place. This is often what emotional outburst, irrational fear or avoidance are about.

We all have immaturity, but most of us just feel shame or embarrassment and try to hide or mask the undeveloped parts of ourselves. We may defend or justify our position, or we might deny or minimize our situation as a way to avoid the discomfort of growing.

Anxiety, depression, addiction, anger, intimacy issues, suicidality, can all be positively affected by inner child work. We may have unresolved anger, pain or fear and we don't know what to do about it. If we don't have the skills and resources to create healthy change, we may just try to avoid or medicate our suffering, rather than taking the hero's journey to face and heal it.

The healing work is to get that child to feel safe and secure. The benefits are developing the confidence, self-compassion and resources to self-parent in a healthy and sustainable way. How we orient to our child self is a metaphor for our emotional and spiritual relationship with ourselves and is a growing internal partnership in present time.

It is important to remember that in *Allies & Demons*, all time is present time. Without this perspective, people may try to connect with their child self part and view it as something historic. They may feel sadness or pity for the child because they know all the things the child will have to live through in the next ten, twenty, or forty years. This is inaccurate because this child is a living part of us today. It is not lost, it's just developmentally frozen in psychological time. Linear time has already passed. We can never re-live the past.

Wounded parts of the self can have profound impact on our lives and we may have no idea. A major disadvantage of cutting off aspects of our self is that we may have a wounded three-year-old or a needy five-year-old who is managing our relationships, our eating habits or our financial life.

For example, my family of origin avoided expressing feelings and emotions. Often vulnerable feelings were ridiculed and I grew to hate raw feelings like sadness, neediness, or fear. When these feelings arose, I felt weak and shameful. I did everything I could to appear as strong and powerful as possible. Consequently, I developed a tough guy mask with a lot of help from drugs and alcohol.

The problem is that I couldn't avoid having vulnerable experiences in life. I'm a super sensitive, emotional person and the vulnerable feelings were still there. I had family, romantic relationships and friendships with people that felt vulnerable, because vulnerability is how we make genuine connection with others. Frequently, when that level of openness came up, I would feel like a defensive four year old. I would be impulsive, reactive or fearful with very little grown up emotional responses to draw from. Sometimes, I couldn't access my adult ego state at all.

It's a powerful practice to be emotionally mindful and ask yourself how old you feel at any given time. If one feels like a child, there is work to be done that will really help mature one's responses. A lot of dysfunctional relationship patterns are driven by the reactions of these inner children. It is usually an attempt to try to heal, but we just don't have the skills or the inner resources.

Often our whole world view is permanently discolored by childhood experiences. This work will bring a shift. It's not about killing the child off or making them go away, it's about taking responsibility for ourselves, developing healthy self-compassion and self-discipline, and bringing all aspects of our self to be part of the larger system. We want to make grown up decisions.

The work of soul retrieval may be understood as going into the transpersonal realm and retrieving an aspect of us that's been frozen in non-ordinary reality. The work is to heal our relationship with these authentic aspects of our self, to integrate the life energy they hold and grow in the ability to treat ourselves with the love, kindness, compassion and even self-discipline that we optimally need.

Soul retrieval is a potent Shamanic technique for integrating separated, lost or disparate parts of the self. Inner child work is a type of soul retrieval. However, soul retrieval can be used to integrate self parts of any age or stage, as we will explore in the following chapters on trauma, depression and anxiety.

People really feel the difference from inner child work. Frequently they will come out of these inner journeys feeling more whole, calm and grounded. They report seeing color more brightly, hearing sound more fully, smelling things more acutely. It's powerful because this is actual power. We are literally adding to our life energy.

## Chloe

Chloe was a tall, quiet young mother who was feeling overwhelmed by her relationship with her new mother-in-law. Angella, the mother-in-law, was a controlling, manipulative woman who had little respect for Chloe. Angella would frequently visit Chloe unexpectedly, often entering the house without knocking.

Chloe, a reserved and private person by nature, was horrified and enraged by Angella's behavior, but was unable to create a healthy boundary or stand up to her mother-in-law. Part of Chloe's anger was that her husband, Tyler, seemed unaffected by her outrage and was unwilling to protect her from his mother's bold behavior.

Chloe grew up with a very sickly mother who was cared for by her father. The family culture was such that anything difficult or frightening was avoided and being sick was a common excuse. Although Chloe had surprised herself with her own strength during childbirth and in her skills as a new mother, she collapsed emotionally in the face of the dominant Angella.

As time passed Chloe grew to hate Angella and began to make excuses, including pretending to be sick to avoid family gatherings. Although Chloe did not want to repeat her childhood family patterns, she had little experience with healthy adult confrontation.

Using Chloe's active imagination and body-centered mindfulness, we went into the feelings of rage and powerlessness associated with Angella. We found Chloe on a couch at the age of ten. Her mother was in a mental hospital for anxiety and anorexia, but the family told the children that their mother was having surgery. Chloe, a very intuitive child, knew that she was being lied to, but she also knew that she could not ask for the truth.

This ten-year-old girl was furious at being made to pretend that mother was physically ill rather than emotionally sick. When we brought this powerful, honest, insightful child into present time, she provided Chloe with a source of strength that she had lost decades before. Her child self was extremely compassionate, but fierce. This child part needed Chloe to tell Angella the truth.

We practiced what Chloe would say and also practiced calling in her guides and teachers for protection and power. Chloe called Angella and simply told her that she would need to call and make arrangements before coming to the house and that she felt very uncomfortable with impromptu visits. Surprisingly, Angella agreed and changed her pattern of dropping by unannounced. In fact, the whole tone of their relationship changed. Chloe didn't like her mother-in-law much better, but she no longer felt bullied or overrun and now knew that she had the resources to stand up for herself and tell the truth in an effective way.

## Healthy Self-Parenting

Most of us are deeply affected by our unresolved emotional issues from childhood. The way our caregivers, teachers, community and peers related to us has a profound impact on how we treat ourselves and interact with the world.

We all develop internal systems to manage our social and emotional experience. These management systems often reflect the type of care we received as children. This isn't meant to blame parents - they were children at one point, too. This is just a developmental fact. We internalize our experience and if that experience was healthy, loving and respectful, we have a healthy internal relationship with our own needs, desires and feelings.

In an optimal child-rearing situation, a child would have most of her needs met by loving parents who accept the child for who she really is and actively support her to be her authentic self. In this environment, the child will naturally internalize the parenting model experienced in their younger years. Then as an adult, the type of successful caregiving received as a child becomes a helpful and even vital internal self part – a healthy self-parent.

If the caregiving was inadequate, as it usually is because everyone is human, then our internal ability to care for ourselves may be flawed and dysfunctional.

For example, Laura's parents were both executives who worked long hours at stressful jobs. Although they cared deeply for Laura and put a lot of resources into her care with nannies, babysitters and extensive after school activities, she didn't actually spend much time with her parents.

As an adult, Laura kept herself extremely busy and was plagued by perfectionism and a need for achievement. She was often the top salesperson at work, ran marathons and trained as a triathlete. No matter how outwardly successful she was, Laura never felt good enough and always pushed herself to achieve more.

Although she was in a long-term relationship with a woman who loved her deeply, Laura was insecure and always feared that she would be abandoned, feelings she kept to herself.

Laura's internal dialogue, her inner parent, constantly pushed her to overachieve in the hopes of finding the love and security she craved. Unfortunately, from an inner child perspective, the part of her that felt inadequate and unloved would never be healed by external success alone.

Life gives us opportunities over and over again to re-pattern our unresolved emotional processes. Intimate relationship, caring for aging parents, death of loved ones and having our own children all provide opportunities for our own wounds to be triggered and ultimately healed. Inner child work is the most direct way I know to shift these deep patterns that are at the root of so much of our suffering and turmoil.

Through the Healing The Child Within journey accompanying this chapter, Laura was able to shift her relationship with her emotional self and develop a compassionate, loving internal parent within. During Laura's inner journey, we connected with her seven-year-old self at ballet class. She had been admonished by the instructor for not having her hair done correctly. Laura had put her own bun in that day, and felt terrible shame and inadequacy. This little girl tried so hard to be brave and independent, but felt she would just never be good enough.

The adult Laura felt tremendous love for this girl and was able to give her inner child a big hug and tell her that the ballet teacher was a jerk and that she was a strong and competent girl who worked really, really hard. The child felt seen and understood.

We brought this lovely little girl out of the ballet studio and to the jungle, where Jaguar, Laura's power animal lived. Laura's adult self felt the immense love, acceptance and grounding presence of Jaguar and was able to tell that girl that she was perfect just the way she was.

Although Laura continued to value high achievement, her internal dialogue shifted and relaxed. Her inner child needed time to just play and enjoy nature, rather than always focusing on outcomes. As she developed a healthy, loving self-parent, Laura was more able to receive the love of her partner and friends and felt an inner security that she had never experienced before.

When we heal our internal relationship with our self, our whole life experience will change. As we approach these child aspects of our self, we find that each child part has had a different experience and will offer us something unique. Some self parts may be brilliant, gifted and full of vitality while others may be sad, lonely, frightened or angry. Regardless of their experience, each part of our self holds essential life energy that is beneficial.

Like Laura, one of the key skills most of us need to develop is healthy self-parenting. Through this work, we cultivate our best adult self and engage directly with long-buried aspects of our past in a helpful way. Through the journey corresponding with this chapter, we can bring these fragmented aspects of who we are into a new sense of integration in the present moment.

## Self Parts

Most people tend to think of themselves as a single cohesive unit or integrated individual personality. My experience as a therapist is that each human being is more like a committee or group than they are a single entity. We are made up of a vast array of life experiences from all phases of our life. We also consist of many emotional, spiritual, social and relational aspects that may be in contrast and even in conflict with each other.

Rather than seeing ourselves as having multiple personality disorder because we have different self parts, the work is to make peace with and integrate our past experience into present time. In *Allies & Demons*, the more concrete we make the various aspects of our self, the more directly we can bring healing and love where it is needed most.

As we recognize, validate and integrate our disparate parts and our past experiences, we find that we become more whole and centered. Our capacity for kindness, compassion and forgiveness grows. We become less rigid, fearful and controlling as we grow in flexibility and presence. Some may find that new creativity flows in. Others may find the courage to pursue goals and dreams that seemed unreasonable or out of reach. Relationships with others deepen as we become more grounded in and directed by our own authentic self. We become less affected and driven by external forces that may not have our best interests at heart.

## Gifts & Talents

Everyone has something to offer the world. We all have gifts and talents. The things that are naturally good about us, we could call our innate intelligence. We all have certain ways we are intelligent, even if we never did well in traditional school.

Multiple intelligence theory insists that there are many different types of intelligence beyond reading, writing, and math. Multiple intelligence theory was developed by Dr. Howard Gardner at Harvard University in the 1980's and is now considered mainstream psychology.

If we expand our concept of intelligence to include the whole human experience, then it is obvious that we can be smart, gifted or talented in many ways: emotional, social, athletic, logical, spatial, relational, to name a few.

Someone might be dyslexic or poor with numbers, but amazing with small children. Another might be a terrific dancer or business manager, but is really challenged by sexual relations or deep emotions. Others might manage conflict with grace but can't find their way around city streets. I have a good friend who quit school in 9th grade and is challenged to write a cohesive sentence or speak with people he doesn't know, but he is one of the best mechanics in town and can fix anything with gears and a motor.

Discovering our inherent abilities is part of owning our unique worth and value as a person. Unfortunately, many of us are disconnected from our best parts or maybe don't even believe they exist.

Think of the world as a garden where we're each a different flower or plant. What if I am born a daffodil, but my family values roses? I want to please my family and try to be a rose. I try to act and smell like a rose, but I am terrible at being a rose because I'm actually a daffodil.

When my daffodil nature pops out or reveals itself in all its glorious yellowness, I feel ashamed and wonder what's wrong with me. Why can't I be a better rose?

This is a human tragedy because I'm a perfectly good daffodil! If I reject my true nature, I will always find myself wishing to be something I am not, rather than developing and rejoicing in who I really am.

Whenever we try to be what we believe we "should" be, we're acting from a place of fear, not our authentic self. The fearful part of us believes we are unlovable as we are. Frequently a false self develops. We could call this our mask self or our ego. Wearing the mask actively disconnects us from our authentic self.

At first this comes into being as a defense, but then it becomes an ingrained, reflexive way of life. Over time, we may lose conscious contact with our authentic self altogether. Even though they can lie dormant for years, our gifts and unique intelligence are always available to us.

As we grow up we don't mature evenly across all the many developmental areas that make us human. The more we illuminate and balance the different aspects of our complex selves, the more successful we'll be in clarifying who we are and evolving in directions we prefer.

Most of us have aspects of our personality where we feel fairly mature and grown-up. These are our personality assets. It's the places where we're under-developed or frozen that inner child work is needed and effective. Through the guided journey accompanying this chapter, we go directly to the wounded or undeveloped child parts to help them grow and mature in a healthy way.

Luckily, the healing and transformation work we do as adults doesn't take the same chronological time that passed when we were developing as children. Healing and recovery can happen exponentially faster when we bring our adult consciousness to immature parts of our self that need to grow, heal and integrate.

Finding, developing and supporting what is good about us is part of healthy self-parenting. Doing so brings a sense of purpose unavailable in other ways.

## Finding His Voice

John was preparing to take voice lessons. He had always sung in the shower and wanted to gain the skills and confidence to do more with his voice. Before his first lesson, John found himself feeling depressed and full of dread. He cancelled the lesson.

In an *Allies & Demons* session, we went into the feeling of dread in his stomach and asked what it was connected to from his past. We came to an experience when John was five and his father shamed him for singing too loudly when Dad was trying to do some work. John never felt "heard" by his father and this experience solidified the idea that he should quiet his voice and he never sang in front of anyone again.

Using our active imagination, we can directly access the child part of ourselves to affect profound transformation and healing in present time. In our sessions, we were able to bring John's best adult self into connection with this wounded five-year-old child and bring the child part out of this traumatic experience where he had been emotionally suffering for much of his life.

John was able to tell this inner child part of himself that it was safe to use his voice and that John, in his adult ego state, was here to love and support this boy in the way he had always needed. This is part of developing a healthy inner parent to replace the shaming, blaming energy he had internalized from his father. After our sessions, John was able to move through his old fear, show up for his lessons and explore his own voice.

We will now connect with wounded, traumatized or neglected aspects of the self using our active imagination. As we help, heal, and re-parent our emotional self in present time, we will find that the most important thing is not what happened to us in the past, but how we relate to these inner parts of ourselves now.

## Emotional Maturity

Our emotions and feelings are a tremendous source of information. They add color, texture and flavor to our lives. Feelings link us with insight and intuition about the choices we need to make on a daily basis. If we lose access to our intuition and our feelings, we lose much of what makes us uniquely human.

Emotional maturity is not lack of feeling. Emotional maturity means being able to process and manage the information coming from our emotional responses. Rather than reacting to our emotions based on habitual past conditioning or just shutting them down entirely, emotional maturity means being able to respond to the outside world and our interior life from a balanced, fully feeling, mindful place.

I think all of us need ongoing work in emotional development and maturity, not just those overtly suffering from emotional trauma. Everyone can benefit from integrating unresolved emotions. As we get more conscious and reflective about the many varied parts of our self, we have greater choice about how we act and react.

Sometimes in life we may need to focus on the task at hand and put aside our feelings. The work is to make time for our feelings later, to process our experience and move on.

Unfortunately, many people operate all the time in this extreme mode of goal oriented actions, maximizing their idealized self-image and suppressing their emotions. They then act out their unfelt emotions unconsciously. They don't know why they got in a fight with their spouse, they don't know why they ended up at the refrigerator eating cookie dough or compulsively playing games on their phone. They tell themselves, "I'm not gonna eat that anymore," but are back at the refrigerator again and again.

Whenever we say, "I don't know why I did that," it's a sign that we need to focus loving attention exactly in that direction. Some aspect of our self is acting out, trying to get our attention. If we push that aspect of our self aside and continue to deny and bury it, it's going to keep acting out – until it gets the attention it needs. This is where self-parenting comes in.

*Allies & Demons* teaches us how to become a responsible self-parent. We aim our parenting attention devotedly toward those childhood parts of ourselves that didn't get their needs met. We can bring unconditional love to parts of ourselves that were misunderstood, ignored or abused. We can bring wisdom and guidance to our own inner child. Now, in the present moment, we are the only ones who can parent our emotional self.

We need to observe inner feelings and outer behavior in our lives that is disruptive and negative from a place of curiosity and compassion. Asking "why" we did something is interesting, but why is usually not a helpful question. We need to ask ourselves what, where and how questions to go deeper into the root of our patterns.

Questions like "What is my motive or drive for this behavior?" or perhaps "Where is this behavior a problem?" or "When did this feeling first start in my life?" provide more useful information.

Through asking the right questions and opening to insight from our guides and inner teachers, we can step by step look deeper into our past, until we come directly to the genesis of an issue. When we heal an issue at its root, many of the presenting problems that developed to protect us from the original pain unravel.

## *Taking The Inner Journey To Heal The Child Within*

The process we will use to heal the child within is a modified Shamanic soul retrieval. This inner journey may be done repeatedly to heal our wounds, develop the ability to parent ourselves in a healthy way and grow in emotional vulnerability and maturity.

> *Guided audio for The Inner Journey To Heal The Child Within is available at www.reneemckenna.com.*

# Get comfortable and take a few deep breaths to relax your body...

*Open your inner senses. Call in your guides, teachers and perhaps the ally you connected with in journey number five. Notice where they are in relation to you.*

*Sense, feel or imagine yourself as a child, perhaps a part of you that needs help or healing right now. How old is this child? This may be a part of you that is sad, hurt, scared, humiliated, distressed or in some kind of suffering.*

*Where is this child? What setting or scene are they in? How are they feeling? What is the child doing?*

*Sense, feel or imagine yourself as you are today, your best adult self, with all the experience you've had and all the work you've done. Bring your guides and teachers with you and imagine stepping into the scene with this child and make yourself known to them.*

*Tell the child we are here to help them. Tell them the situation they are in happened a long time ago, they don't need to live there anymore. Tell them we're here to bring them into present time so they can be loved and cared for in the way they've always needed. They don't need to be alone anymore.*

*How is it for the child to hear this? Does the child know who you are? If they don't, you might tell them that you are their adult self here to help them.*

*How do your guides and teachers feel about this child? Is the child aware of them? How do they feel about the guides and teachers?*

*How do you feel about this child? How does this child feel about you?*

*How have you related with or treated this child part of yourself in your life? If you've ignored or been unaware of this part of yourself, what effect has this had on this child? Is there anything you'd like to do or communicate with the child? What does this child need from you?*

*Ask if they are willing to have a little outing. We want to bring them out of this historic situation which, you can remind them, happened a long time ago. They don't need to live there anymore. We want to bring them to a powerful, safe, sacred space in nature that has only their highest good in mind.*

*Bring this child to a safe and powerful place in nature right now. It may be a place you've been before or someplace new. Your guides and teachers can assist with this.*

*How is it for the child to be in this natural place? Assure them that no one can come here without their permission and that anything that happens here is a teaching for them for their own development and highest good. They can do whatever they want here - rest, explore, play or get dirty.*

*Notice how the child feels in this place as they become more aware of what's around them. Do they hear or smell anything? Is it day or night? What are the elements in this place? What are the colors and textures? What is the quality of the air?*

*As the child becomes more aware of this place, they might become aware that the spirit of this place is aware of them and is even glad that they have come. How is it for the child to open to this deep connection with nature?*

*Is there anything in particular that the child feels drawn to or that seems drawn to them? The child can make this connection right now. How does it feel to be connected in this way in a place of compassion, power, wisdom and support? Assure them that they are safe in this place.*

*Bring your awareness to the child. What's good about them? What are their gifts, talents and attributes? Is this child creative? Sensitive? Are they discerning, brave, compassionate, smart, adventurous, innocent, open or vulnerable?*

*How might you benefit from connecting with this energy in your own life now? Is there anything you'd need to do or change to make room for this child part of yourself in your life today?*

*Are you willing to care for and love this child in the way they've always needed? This is a living relationship and your guides and teachers can help you grow in caring and supporting this aspect of yourself.*

*Ask the child if they want to stay in this place in nature or do they want to be with you in your life today? It's up to the child, but know that you'll have access to them whatever their choice is. The ultimate goal is for them to come and be with you, but they can do that when they're ready.*

*If the child does want to be with you, hug the child into your body, breathing them in physically, mentally, emotionally, spiritually, energetically, sexually, relationally and creatively. You might even feel a filling sensation as you retrieve this aspect of your own soul energy into you.*

*Bringing this child back makes you more whole than you have ever been. Integrating them in this way invites their attributes to combine with your own. You now have access to their gifts, talents and life energy more than ever before. Breathe the child in and welcome them home. Sense, feel or imagine their being flowing all the way down to the soles of your feet, out to your fingertips and up to the crown of your head, integrating into every system of your body, adding to your own life force.*

*When this feels complete, ask your guides and teachers if there is anything else that wants to be done or communicated. If the child wants to stay in nature, they're welcome to, knowing they are safe and supported. Your guides and teachers can stay there with them in their spirit aspect.*

*When you're ready, bring all of this back with you into your body. Remembering everything fully, open your eyes when you feel ready. Take a moment and check in on that child. Notice where they are in relation to you in the room or in the place in nature. How is the child feeling? How does it feel to be connected with them in this way?*

*Write down your experience in a journal or notebook.*

## CHAPTER 7

# Transforming Trauma

*I would rather be whole than good.*
- CARL JUNG

Trauma is the Greek word for wound. Most people have unresolved wounding from their past. A wound in *Allies & Demons* is an emotional, mental, spiritual, physical, sexual, social or energetic experience that remains unhealed. The inner journeys related with the next two chapters provide powerful new pathways for healing the demons of trauma, abuse and neglect.

When an incoming experience is too much to handle and the psyche is unable to process or integrate the event in a manageable way, trauma happens. Part of us just can't or won't believe what is happening and there is a disconnection, a shattering or splintering of the self in an attempt to manage reality and not go crazy.

Trauma can be the result of a single event like an accident, a surgery, an unexpected loss, or being physically, sexually or psychologically harmed. Trauma can also result from chronic, long-term stress or dysfunction, like war, incarceration, hospitalization, abuse, neglect or bullying. Birth trauma, both for the mother and the newborn, is extremely common and unrecognized in most psychological modalities.

What happens with a physical injury is not that different from what happens when we are harmed emotionally, mentally or spiritually. When the body is wounded there is a breach in the usual systems we have for protection like skin, muscle and bones. Immediately after an injury the body moves into healing mode automatically to protect and mend the wound.

First there is pain to let us know there is a problem. Then there is swelling, as blood rushes to repair and protect the injured area. A vast array of specialized blood cells work to clear dead and damaged tissue while new growth takes place. The area stays sore so that we protect it while it heals. The immune system is often on high alert during this process, looking for intruders. Over time the bone will reform itself, the skin will mend by forming scabs and scar tissue.

In the same way that the body goes into high alert to focus on protecting and healing a physical injury, the psyche has a complex system to manage overload as well. Just as the body goes into shock as a way to save itself, the mind and emotions can go into shock during and after a traumatic event.

Similar to how the body sends all of its protective resources to deal with healing wounds of the flesh through swelling, immune function and pain, so the mind and emotions will focus their energy on survival first and then on regaining balance and normal function later.

## Integrating The Traumatized Self

Trauma responses differ between people, but the basic issue is the splitting or separating of the inner self in response to the traumatic event. In an attempt to manage the unmanageable, the psyche does something quite brilliant. Like an ejection seat, the emotional part of the self experiencing the trauma can be split off, separated from the rational mind or left behind to ensure survival.

Just as an oyster creates a pearl when a piece of sand or other damaging irritant gets inside their shell, our psyche encases the traumatized part of the self in an energetic state of denial and resistance. This inner separation is an automatic response, not a decision.

This encasement of the wounded self is a survival mechanism that works well in the short run, but causes problems in the long run because the traumatized self part usually remains separated and stuck. It remains separate because this inner splitting happens unconsciously. Therefore nothing is done to reintegrate the traumatized self part after the event.

Healing trauma in *Allies & Demons* means to return these split or fractured parts of the self to health and wholeness in present time, using the soul retrieval process accompanying this chapter. Soul retrieval for trauma is similar to the journey we did to heal the inner child in Chapter 6.

Most difficult life experiences will heal naturally over time, similar to physical healing. If there is a death, loss, life crisis or accident, emotional or mental pain lets us know we need to care for ourselves.

Grief is one of the natural, healthy ways of processing, letting go of the past and opening to new experience. The stages of grief can apply to any major change in our lives, not just to the loss of death.

Elisabeth Kübler-Ross in her 1969 book *On Death and Dying* named five stages of grief and loss she observed: denial, anger, bargaining, depression and acceptance. Each stage is an internal coping skill or processing tool. Because each person copes with change in a unique way, these stages may be experienced in different orders with some skipped entirely. There is no correct way to deal with grief, trauma or major change.

If we allow ourselves to move fully through our organic emotional, mental and spiritual process, we will come out the other side stronger and more resilient. Scar tissue is tougher than skin and healed bone is thicker at the site of a break. Healing is possible but we may need help.

Life changes us if we submit ourselves to it. Allowing ourselves to be changed by the events and adventures of life is part of our evolution. Accepting and surrendering to our unique life process, no matter how challenging, is our work. Resistance to the often difficult experience of reality is what causes problems.

When we face and accept what is, we participate in the evolutionary flow of life. Resisting reality causes suffering. Though resisting pain is understandable, we can't cheat the circumstances of our life, no matter how difficult. The only way out is through. It is only through deeply living and feeling our own experience that we grow and mature as life calls us to do.

Life is constant change. How we react or respond to the constant flow of change life presents is our choice. Our daily choices create our reality.

There is a natural healing process for the non-physical effects of shocking or damaging experiences. Emotional distress, mental anguish and spiritual distrust or disconnection can and should be repaired. Healing is a growing, strengthening process. Like healing of physical injury, it can be uncomfortable. We need to care for ourselves in special ways so that healing can take place, just as we might need to walk on crutches while a bone mends.

In *Allies & Demons*, we assist the healing process by first grounding in spiritual help, which is like going to the ER or the doctor. Then we make internal adjustments similar to resetting a broken bone or stitching a cut, by doing the journeys for healing trauma that relate with these next two chapters, found online at www.reneemckenna.com.

We may need to reclaim important life energy lost in the trauma similar to receiving a blood transfusion, eating healthy foods or taking vitamins or medicine. We rest and allow the natural balance of our systems to return, as we would keep our arm in a sling or bandage a wound.

Our body/mind complex will heal naturally if we create the right conditions. The Universe conspires to help us. Patience and persistence are key. We may need some rehab to regain lost strength after an injury. Psychologically and spiritually we may need to make changes to how we understand or move through the world after a traumatic event, like strengthening muscles after a knee replacement or learning to walk after a stroke.

Life is always calling us to grow and our life experiences are the language of this call. Like healing from physical injury takes time, recovering from psycho-spiritual trauma can be a long process. It is common to want to deny or resist the emotional, mental and spiritual healing needed in any given situation. Unfortunately, resistance keeps us stuck in the very suffering we are trying to avoid.

## Deadly Crash

Theresa, a forty-something interior designer from England, suffered from chronic fatigue and anxiety. As we explored the genesis of her symptoms, she recalled a terrible train wreck she had experienced in her early 20's in Britain.

I had to ask many questions to get Theresa to talk about this terrible event. She spent years trying not to think about it. She had nightmares in the months following the crash and had taken sleeping pills nightly ever since.

Following her body-felt experience of anxiety and her active imagination, we found Theresa wandering through the horrific aftermath of a massive train crash. She walked numbly past dead and bleeding passengers, her own arm broken.

With the help of her guides and teachers we brought this traumatized part of Theresa out of the crash scene and into her sacred place, a private English garden surrounded by a tall hedge. Theresa felt guilty for having survived an accident where many of her fellow passengers died. A deeply compassionate person, she felt awful for not being able to help, but was able to see that she had been seriously wounded. Overcome with pain and shock, she had been barely capable of escaping the wreckage herself. The wounded part of Theresa collapsed on the grass in her sacred garden and received healing energy from the earth and sun.

Theresa was able to forgive the traumatized part of herself, but still deeply felt the presence of two passengers who died that day. The day of the crash, she walked past their bodies and now felt compelled to help them in her inner journey.

Grounding with her teacher in human form, the archangel Michael, we were able to contact the spirits of these dead passengers. The dead, a young man and an older woman, had attached themselves to Theresa in her traumatized state.

Working with the dead is deeply healing and advanced work in *Allies & Demons* known as spirit release or psychopomp. With the guidance of her spiritual teacher, we were able to call in a portal of light and the dead spirits were able to pass into the next place.

Before their release, Theresa told them she was sorry that she had not been able to help them. The young man didn't fully understand that he had died and was attended to by his ancestors who came through the light to help him. The older woman expressed remorse for having attached herself to Theresa unknowingly.

Following this profound inner journey, Theresa's anxiety lessened considerably and she regained a level of energy she hadn't felt since her twenties. She stopped taking sleeping pills and began to learn about meditation and to explore psychic phenomenon, a field which had always interested her.

In *Allies & Demons* we focus on finding and healing the root of an issue. The root of trauma is often found in our relationship with ourselves, particularly the part of us that is vulnerable, frightened and hurt. Attending to wounded parts of ourselves with compassion, love and understanding is profoundly healing. When the core issue is transformed, the symptoms resolve themselves because there is nothing driving them.

## Denial & Resistance

Frequently after a traumatic event, we want to just get on with life and hope to remain unaffected. We may try to forgo the internal work that is necessary to make everything functional again. This is the root of resistance.

Although resistance to authentic pain is understandable, resistance actually causes more problems in the long run because it blocks real healing and integration from happening. What we resist persists and resistance is a type of avoidance. By avoiding our trauma, we end up perpetuating it, because the underlying emotional material remains stuck or unresolved.

We may develop magical thinking and hope to wish the trauma away and bypass the important inner work either because we don't know what to do or we don't have faith that healing is possible. Trauma to the psyche requires extra attention and focus that isn't widely understood by our very physically-centered worldview. Whatever the cause, resistance is at the root of trauma and can keep us stuck in suffering indefinitely.

There is a very fine line to walk here. No one chooses trauma. Yet healing from trauma pushes us to grow in consciousness, courage and trust in life and ourselves on the deepest levels. The difference between a difficult experience and a trauma is the level of resistance to what happened. True healing must include an acceptance of the reality of an experience. Trauma is generally caused by a particular kind of denial. We could call it traumatic denial.

Avoiding the horror of an accident, the terror of being attacked or the shock of witnessing violence is totally understandable. Trauma is a coping skill. Often people come to therapy seeking relief from the secondary symptoms of unresolved emotional experience such as anxiety, depression, addiction, insomnia and phobias. Much of Western psychology focuses on relieving these symptoms, yet leaves the underlying trauma unresolved.

## Jose's Story

As my client Jose walked to his car one night after leaving the gay bar he frequented, he was attacked by a group of men and robbed. Jose was a muscular construction worker who had rarely lost a fight because of his stature. He went to the hospital and got checked out. He had some serious bruises, but was basically okay. He took a few days off of work and then resumed his regular routine.

Jose remained shaken, but seemed alright for the first few weeks after the event, then he started to have nightmares. He tried to shake off these experiences and power through, then one afternoon he had a panic attack in the parking lot of a supermarket. He was overcome with a racing pulse and cold sweats, seemingly out of nowhere. These frightening episodes happened more frequently and Jose became afraid to leave the house or go to sleep, fearing more nightmares or panic. It really freaked him out. His partner called to make an appointment for him, as his machismo was preventing Jose from getting the help he needed.

When he came to see me, he was having trouble getting to work, was sleep-deprived and distraught. Through the soul retrieval journey at the end of this chapter, we were able to repattern his experience of the terrible encounter.

Using Jose's active imagination, we found the part of him that had been attacked that night lying dazed and bleeding in the parking lot. His traumatized self felt ashamed that he had "allowed" this gay-bashing to happen. He had lived as an openly gay man in San Francisco for most of his adult life and his sense of personal power and safety was shattered.

As we helped this injured part of him, Jose was forced to open to his own vulnerability and powerlessness. He told this traumatized self part that the attack was not his fault and that there was nothing he could have done to prevent it. Releasing his shame for being attacked was emotional and palpable as Jose forgave himself and accepted that he had been victimized.

In the weeks that followed, his panic attacks and nightmares stopped and his life returned to normal. However, Jose continued to do work in *Allies & Demons* for another six months seeking to grow in open-heartedness and compassion.

There was another layer of healing for Jose called power retrieval where he took back the life energy that was stolen by the men who attacked him. This is important work and we will learn more about power retrieval in Chapter 8.

## Return To Wholeness

If you think about a person like a house that is wired for electricity, we have multiple wires that power our different circuits. The wires move electrical current or life energy to our body parts, but also to our emotional, mental, spiritual and energetic systems.

Anybody who has ever plugged anything in knows that if you unplug a lamp it doesn't work anymore. The lamp is not broken, it just doesn't have access to the current it needs to light up. You can always plug it back in.

Extreme emotional, mental or physical overload can have an internal effect similar to unplugging an appliance, blowing a fuse or tripping the breaker switch. Once a fuse is blown, all those things that were plugged into that area of the house are still there, but they are unavailable because they don't have power. They aren't able to turn on because that circuit breaker shut down.

The reason a fuse exists is so the house doesn't catch fire. It's actually a safety valve, a really important system. Similarly, internal splitting is a survival tool for the psyche, a brilliant protective mechanism.

Unfortunately, because internal splitting isn't a recognized psychological phenomenon, nothing is done to reverse the process. The split-off self part never gets returned, power is never restored and we may even develop a new line of defenses and compensations to make up for the parts we have lost access to.

Soul retrieval resets our spiritual breaker and restores power to the house. The work is to reclaim the self parts and life energy that were split off or lost in the trauma. We make it safe to bring the traumatized self part out of the distressing event and into present time. *Allies & Demons is not about re-experiencing the traumatic event.* It's actually about releasing past trauma, integrating reality, coming fully into present time and becoming whole.

What happens with trauma is that the aspect of the self that had the shocking experience gets cut off from the rest of the psyche. It never goes away because it is a part of the life force, but it becomes unavailable, separated or abandoned, similar to what happens with the wounded inner child from Chapter 6.

Sometimes people consciously avoid anything that reminds them of the original situation in an attempt to manage their trauma. For others, entire periods of time can be pushed into the unconscious. I have clients who have no memory of their childhood before the age of 13. They don't remember anything. This is called traumatic memory loss.

Whether through avoidance, denial or memory loss, the traumatized person may lose access to essential parts of their own life energy. Part of their life force becomes unavailable or inaccessible. This energy loss may go unnoticed or the person may attribute their fatigue, lack of motivation and general malaise to depression. Some may lose interest in work, relationships, hobbies, or even lose the will to live.

Anxiety and panic attacks are common symptoms of unintegrated trauma. Panic and anxiety can be understood as the fragmented parts of the self trying to reconnect back to the whole. Like lost children locked outside, they bang on the door of consciousness through intrusive dreams, anxiety and panic attacks trying to get our attention.

From the perspective of *Allies & Demons*, life energy is quantifiable, even if we do not have the means to measure it yet. When aspects of the self are fractured, they carry with them important parts of the host from which they came. Unfortunately, some of the best of who we are can become unavailable to us through traumatic splitting or shattering of the self.

We may lose our creativity, spontaneity, curiosity, innocence or sexuality. Because the essence of life energy is positive and constructive, all parts of the self - even parts that are wounded or traumatized - hold vital, beneficial life energy.

Unfortunately, unresolved trauma tends to create and reinforce destructive formations like fear, anger, victimhood or shutting down. These are defenses that may form to support resistance and denial or they may grow to replace or fill in the authentic life energy that was lost.

Many people have their memories intact and are actively trying to heal through talk therapy and other means. Talk therapy can be really helpful in understanding what happened, but it may have limited effect on trauma because it is the spiritual and energetic systems that are damaged. Until a repair is done on this soul level, symptoms will often remain.

The brain cannot effect change on a soul level, just as the heart can't breathe and lungs can't digest food. Each organ, each system in the self, has its own important function and its own healing wisdom. When accessed directly, great change is possible, but we need to know where to bring the work and what tools to use.

Sometimes rather than one part of the self splitting off, there is an effect like a shattering of the self. Depending on the person, the severity of the experience or repetitive trauma, like ongoing sexual, physical or emotional abuse, the person's sense of themselves may get smashed. The usual mental and emotional coping strategies break down. This is one way to understand a mental breakdown.

In these cases, the core repair work is the same, to return the lost parts of the self to wholeness. However, there may be multiple self parts to gather and restore, many readjustments to make and a longer time to rehabilitate. Healing from long-term trauma is totally possible, but it takes time and effort.

If you think again about the house metaphor, we don't get to use the computer, lights or microwave that are in that part of the house with no power. In our case this means that we don't have access to all the gifts and talents that the self holds. Every part of us carries essential life energy. When we split off or shut down, we lose access to our own authentic power.

In a house we replace the blown fuse. In the self, we retrieve or return the soul or self part that was cut off. In this way, we literally have more life energy. This energy becomes available to us in present time, bringing us to greater wholeness and personal power, allowing us to leave the traumatic event in the past where it belongs.

From this perspective, many of the symptoms of Post Traumatic Stress Disorder - anxiety, depression, nightmares, panic attacks -

can be understood as parts of the self trying to reconnect with the whole. Unfortunately, they can remain outside of our consciousness for years.

Self part integration is the most powerful and effective way that I know of healing the symptoms of trauma. I would not be a fully functioning person today if it were not for inner self part work.

It must be noted that physical illness or injury, surgery, giving birth, being born, living in constant worry or fear, major depression, long-term depression or anxiety, divorce, getting married, getting fired, changing jobs, moving, death - even the death of someone you don't know personally, can all result in trauma.

The sad thing is that we have unrealistic expectations that we "should" feel a certain way. When our feelings or experience don't match with our idealized expectations, then we may shame or blame ourselves for being human. Then we have two problems. We have the actual unresolved distress and then we have the internal blame and shame on top of it. More layers may be added as time goes on. This is how issues get buried and go unresolved.

## Rachel's Story

As a teenage virgin, Rachel was raped on the beach during a date. She didn't know the boy very well, but had a crush on him and was thrilled to be asked out. As he forced himself on her, she had the experience of leaving her body and watching the rape as if she were floating above the scene.

The boy drove her home and she told no one what had happened. She remained in a floaty state on and off for years. Her grades dropped. She lost interest in social events and only dated men she didn't like very much. Her inner narrative was that the rape was her fault. She should have known better and vowed never to be vulnerable again. This is known as dissociation.

In *Allies & Demons*, dissociation is literal. Rachel actually split off part of herself during the rape. This inner splitting was her psyche's response to the trauma, just as the body might go into shock.

Rachel remained in a state of semi-shock for years. She eventually went to talk therapy, discussed the rape and got on some psych meds that helped a little. The deeper issue, the ongoing trauma, was caused by the internal split and self-blame.

At least two things happened here to create long-term trauma. First, Rachel dissociated or left her body as a way to cope with the horror of the sexual assault. Then she blamed herself for what had happened. There are often many layers of traumatic denial and separation from the vulnerable self part that lived through the trauma.

How we relate with our own vulnerability is key to wholeness and health. Some may lose access to memories completely or try to deny their wounded self, others may shame, blame, reject or even hate their wounded, dissociated parts.

Ultimately, most personal growth and transformation happens through healing our relationship with ourselves, particularly parts that hold painful memories. Bringing our best adult self into relationship with our wounds is transformative. By validating and integrating our vulnerable self, we are able to release the trauma response and put the past behind us. We can then live more fully and authentically in the present.

When we resist or deny our experience, then it solidifies. Rather than moving forward in a healthy flow, we become stuck and stagnant. New layers of traumatic denial may develop as our resistance grows.

It is shocking to see a friend killed on a battlefield, to be beaten by a caregiver or to lose a cherished loved one. We don't want these things to be true. Beyond that, we often don't have the capacity to take in what is happening at the time.

One aspect of trauma is that the experience confronts our understanding of reality. It may seem preferable to split off rather than internalize the truth. How does one process that grandma is a sexual predator or that death is always at our door?

The inner splitting Rachel experienced is called soul loss and the effects are devastating. The part of Rachel that separated out during the rape - her innocent, vulnerable, hopeful, curious self - remained cut off from the rest of her. She was unwhole and no amount of intellectual discussion would heal that divide.

Through the powerful process of soul retrieval, we were able to find, care for and return this lost self part to Rachel. During the inner journey we found the traumatized part of Rachel on the beach where she was raped. This self part presented as teenage Rachel on the night of the event. When adult Rachel imagined herself stepping into the scene with this younger part of herself, the younger, traumatized part didn't recognize Rachel from present time. This younger part had been frozen in this terrible situation, in a state of perpetual trauma for years.

With the help of her guides and teachers, we got the teenage Rachel off of the beach and brought her to her sacred place in nature, a warm and sunny meadow. We explained that we were here to help her and that she didn't need to be alone anymore and that she was safe now, in present time.

The younger Rachel collapsed onto the grass and sobbed and sobbed. The energy of the sun absorbed into her skin to warm her and her power animal, a crow, flew to her side. As the girl calmed down and grounded herself in the sacred place, we explained that time had passed and shared some life events that had happened to Rachel since the rape to help integrate this teenage girl.

From this clear place, both parts of Rachel were able to see that the rape was not her fault. Her self-blame turned to compassion and she forgave her younger self for what happened and agreed to love and care for this part of herself that had been lost for so long.

By bringing this innocent soul part into present time using Rachel's active imagination, she re-integrated her own sense of innocence, curiosity and life energy back to its true home within herself. She shifted from victim to survivor. Over time, the rape became part of her past rather than something she had to defend herself from every day. She was able to process the rape experience and make some clear decisions about how to stay safe with men. Rachel no longer approached intimate relationship from a place of fear and self-rejection, but from a place of empowerment and wholeness.

# *Taking The Inner Journey To Transform Trauma*

The following inner journey is NOT about re-experiencing trauma. This session focuses on rescuing, retrieving and reintegrating valuable parts of the self that were lost or disconnected as the result of trauma. We already lived through the traumatic experience once. There is no value in living through it again. In fact, one way to understand trauma, is that a part of us is actually stuck in the distressing event. Our work is to bring the parts of ourself out of the traumatic experience and into present time, where they can heal, recover and receive what they need from our guides and teachers and our own highest self.

Whether you believe that you experienced trauma or not, this inner journey can be used to process unresolved emotional issues, producing greater wholeness and inner peace. This inner journey may be done repeatedly to heal, restore and integrate wounded parts of the self.

*You may listen to the guided audio for the Inner Journey To Transform Trauma at www.reneemckenna.com.*

# *Find a place to sit or lie down...*

Take a few deep breaths to relax your body and get comfortable. With each breath let your awareness drop deeper into your own inner world. Call in the guides and allies you have connected with in previous journeys. See which allies want to be present to bring insight and information to the traumatized or wounded part of yourself that need help.

Notice where this spiritual help is in relation to you. Do the guides and allies create a particular configuration around you? Notice how it feels to have that energy here with you right now.

Sense, feel or imagine the part of yourself that needs help right now. We are seeking a part of you that experienced trauma, abuse or neglect. We are here to help this part of yourself so that they don't have to suffer anymore. If you experienced a particular trauma, imagine the part of yourself that experienced the trauma or shock.

How old is this part of yourself? What is their setting? Where are they? What's the scene they're in - is it day or night? How are they feeling? What are they doing?

Imagine yourself as you are today, your best adult self with all the experience you've had and all the work you've done. Bring your guides and teachers with you and imagine, sense or feel yourself stepping into the scene with this part of yourself and making yourself known to them. Tell them we are here to help. Tell them the situation they are in happened a long time ago and they don't need to live there anymore. Tell them we're here to bring them into present time so they can heal and be loved and cared for in the way they've always needed. Tell them they don't need to be alone anymore.

How is it for this part of yourself to hear this? Do they know who you are? If they don't communicate, tell them now that you are their adult self from present time here to help them.

*How do your guides and teachers feel about this part of you? How do they feel about your guides and teachers? How do you feel about this wounded part of yourself? How does this wounded part feel about you?*

*How have you related with this part of yourself in your life? How have you treated your abused, traumatized or neglected self? If you've ignored or been unaware of this part of yourself, what effect has this had on them? Is there anything you'd like to do or communicate with this wounded self part right now? What do they need in general? What do they need? Can you or your allies provide this for them now?*

*Ask this part if they are willing to leave this place? We want to bring them out of this historic situation which, you can remind them, happened a long time ago. They don't need to live there anymore. We want to bring them into present time. We want to bring them to a safe and sacred space in nature that has only their highest good in mind.*

*Bring this part of you to a beautiful and powerful place in nature right now. It may be a place you've been before or someplace new. Your allies can assist with this if needed.*

*How is it for them to be in this place in nature? Assure them that no one can come to this place without their permission. Anything that happens here is a teaching for their own development and highest good.*

*They can do whatever they want or need to make themselves comfortable - they can rest, explore, receive healing or interact with the elements here.*

*Notice how this part of yourself feels in this place as they become more aware of what's around them. Do they hear or smell anything? Is it day or night? What are the elements in this place? What are the colors and textures? What is the quality of the air?*

*As they become more aware of this place, they might become aware that the spirit of this place is aware of them and is perhaps glad that they have come. How is it for them to open to this deep connection with nature?*

Is there anything in particular that they feel drawn to or that seems drawn to them? How does it feel for them to be connected in this way in a place of compassion, power, wisdom and support? Assure them that they are safe in this place.

Are you willing to care for and love this part of you in the way they've always needed? This is a living relationship and your guides and teachers can help you grow in caring for and supporting this aspect of yourself.

Assure this part of yourself that they are in present time now and they need never return to the place of trauma where you found them, unless they want to go back. They are in a safe place that has only their healing and evolution as its focus. How is it for them to hear this?

Ask them if they want to stay in this place in nature to heal and recover or come and be with you in your life today? It's up to them, but know that you'll have access to them whatever their choice is. The ultimate goal is for them to come and be with you, but they can do that when they're ready.

If they do want to be with you, sense, feel or imagine hugging them into your body, breathing them in physically, mentally, emotionally, spiritually, energetically, sexually, socially, relationally, professionally and creatively. You might even feel a filling sensation as you retrieve this aspect of your own soul energy into you.

Breathe them in and welcome them home. Imagine their being flowing all the way down the soles of your feet, out to your fingertips and up to the crown of your head, integrating them into every system of your body, adding to your own life force.

When this feels complete, ask your guides and teachers if there is anything else that wants to be done or communicated. If this part of yourself wants to stay in this place, they're welcome to, knowing they are safe and supported. You'll be able to be aware of them and check in on them more easily than ever before. Your guides and teachers can *stay there with them in their spirit aspect and they will receive the compassion and healing they need here.*

*Remembering everything fully, come back into your body, mind, emotions and spirit. Take all the time you need and open your eyes when you feel ready.*

*Check in with the part of you that we just connected with. Notice where they are in relation to you in the room. How are they feeling?*

*You might want to take a few moments and write down your experience in a journal or your Allies & Demons Workbook.*

## CHAPTER 8

# Reclaiming Lost Power

*Truth is the ultimate power. When the truth comes around, all the lies have to run and hide.*

- Ice Cube

Trauma doesn't have to be a one time event. Repetitive long-term distress, like neglect, verbal, physical or sexual abuse, or long-term physical illness can cut people off from themselves to great detriment. Certainly, witnessing or experiencing a terrible event can shock someone and blow their fuse. Over time, one can also be depleted drip by drip until the bucket is empty.

Abuse or neglect that happens over a long period of time can have devastating consequences, as a person is separated over and over from their life energy.

## Rebuilding The Self

Dori, an Emergency Room nurse, was incredible under pressure and dealt with life and death issues calmly, with great compassion and confidence. She was a self-described overachiever who had perpetual anxiety about her performance, although she was a prized employee at nearly every hospital she worked for.

Dori's mom died of cancer when she was 11. Her father was a Vietnam veteran, who was terribly scarred in a war accident, both internally and externally. His deforming facial scars reflected the torment and rage he brought home from the war.

As Dori's mom got sicker, her father Jeff became angrier and more abusive. One day, Dori had an argument with him about cleaning her room. Jeff frequently acted like a drill sergeant who expected the house to be spotless. On this day Dori's room was particularly messy. In a fit of rage, her father yelled that her mom was dying because Dori was a bad kid. This insane comment embedded itself in her eleven-year-old brain and became a driving force in her life.

Dori tried everything she could think of to "be good" so that her mom would get better. She got A's in school, played sports and worked around the house cleaning and cooking. Dori never felt good enough, no matter what she achieved.

After her mother died, she felt a tremendous sense of failure. Her father's rage was unpredictable, as was his drinking. Dori made dinner frequently and cleaned as best she could. If her cooking pleased Jeff, all was well. If he drank too much or the spaghetti was over-cooked, the plate might end up being thrown against the wall or she herself might get thrown against the wall. The worst part was that she had no one to talk to about what was happening.

People deal with the trauma in their lives in many, many different ways. For Dori, it was to try as hard as she could to help people and to be perfect in anything she did. Dori excelled at outdoor sports and became ski patrol and a professional level rock climber. She worked as a flight nurse of an emergency medical helicopter team. She knew trauma intimately and dedicated her work life to helping others survive it. But she had a truckload of her own unresolved trauma that slowly caught up with her.

Dori developed a prescription drug problem to manage her anxiety and insomnia. She often forgot to eat or care for herself and had a long history of relationships with men who were addicts and alcoholics.

After Dori got sober, she started to have trauma symptoms and began to work with a therapist. After a particularly difficult break up, she was overcome with debilitating grief and started to do work in *Allies & Demons*.

From a spiritual perspective Dori had been stripped over and over on an energetic level. Soul retrieval for long-term abuse and trauma is a rebuilding experience, like discussed in Chapter 7. Layer after layer of the self is returned and integrated. This takes time, but the results are dynamic and powerful.

We did many soul retrievals to heal Dori's wounds from the extensive abuse of her father and to process the loss of her mother. One particularly poignant process brought us to Dori a few months after her mother had passed. We approached Dori as a 12-year-old girl in her childhood bedroom. She was drawing a picture of her mother and writing the words breast cancer in pretty colors in a sketchbook she kept under her bed.

Her father Jeff entered her room and flew into a rage at seeing the artwork.

"We don't talk about breast cancer!" He screamed as he tore the book from her hands and stormed out of the room. She sobbed on her bed and never saw the notebook again.

Using Dori's active imagination, we brought her guides and teachers into the room with this grieving girl. Dori hugged her younger self and they cried together.

Dori was able to communicate to this abused and traumatized child that her dad was crazy and that she didn't need to be alone with her feelings anymore. We told the girl that this awful situation happened a long time ago and she didn't need to live in that place anymore, that we were here to bring her into present time where she would be loved and cared for in the way she really needed.

We brought younger Dori to her sacred place by the ocean and connected her with Octopus, her loving, motherly power animal. Dori took the girl's face in her hands, looked deep into her eyes and told her that her mother died of breast cancer and that it was not her fault.

The girl slumped into the arms of her adult self in relief and Octopus stroked her hair.

When I asked what was good about this girl, Dori was quiet for a moment.

"She's a really, really good kid. She's such a good kid. She tried so hard and she really cares about people. I don't think I've ever really seen her before. She's so strong. She went through so much and she did it, she did everything really well. She's pretty amazing," Dori cried and hugged this girl hard.

For the first time in her life, her abused self felt seen, appreciated and loved. She had received many compliments and accolades over the years, but always deflected them.

In acknowledging her own inner value, Dori began to see herself more accurately and to own her accomplishments and strengths. She grew in confidence and lost the constant driving need to push and prove herself. She developed a rich internal sense of self love and value, something she had always sought externally which was never enough.

It was important to recover the power Dori lost in the years of abuse from her father. Jeff died years before, but we were able to call the energy of his highest self to a space where Dori's guides brought us for power retrieval, a tropical rainforest. Jeff appeared as a younger version of himself, still scarred from his war experience, but before her mother had died.

Dori didn't want to interact with Jeff. He was rather numb and lifeless. Through her power retrieval guide, a wise and radiant woman, Dori told her father she wanted her power back. He had treated her badly and she needed to move on. Jeff nodded blankly as her guide gathered the clear light of Dori's life energy from Jeff and transmitted it into Dori's throat and heart.

Radiant Woman, Dori's guide, then took the war trauma, grief and disappointment that she had taken on from her father and returned it to him. As a child, Dori recalled being woken up by her father yelling in his sleep. Jeff had his own trauma, she knew; he acted out and shut down rather than getting help.

Dori had a sense of understanding for Jeff, but after the session she said, "He's still an asshole. I'm glad he's gone."

Dori continues to do inner work to heal her layers of trauma. Over time she decided to leave her stressful work as a flight nurse and took a position which allows her to spend more time in nature, mountain biking and rock climbing. She has come to value and respect the part of herself who lived through the trauma of her early years. She has an attitude of self-love and self-care which she formerly reserved only for her patients.

## Collective Trauma

Terrorism, war, famine, earthquakes, floods or industrial accidents can ravage individuals and whole societies. The aftermath of collective trauma can cause suffering for decades, being passed through generations as it was between Jeff and Dori. Slavery has left a devastating legacy of trauma in African American culture. The Jewish

Holocaust of the 20th century and the Native American genocide of the 19th Century continue to haunt these communities today.

The soul retrieval work offered in the previous chapter may have to be done repeatedly to integrate all the layers of a person's separated or fragmented psyche resulting from personal or collective trauma.

We have much work to do as a species to heal our collective trauma. However, healing usually starts with ourselves first. When we heal ourselves, our intrinsic connection with all of consciousness affects positive change. As we resonate on a higher level, we elevate the resonance for everyone.

## Soul Stealing

In Chapter 7 we met Jose and Rachel, who both suffered violent attacks. This is a particular type of trauma that has a layer of complexity that accidents or natural disasters don't have, which is the negative intention of the person perpetrating the harm.

On a soul level, when one person intentionally harms another, they are stealing the life energy of their victim. Parents may feel completely justified in beating their children or handing out constant biting criticism. Romantic partners may believe it is their right to force sexual relations on a spouse or lover and never call it rape. It's considered a soldier's duty to take enemy lives in battle. Thieves have no respect for the rights or property of others. It is fairly well known that bullying is an attempt to inflate oneself by deflating another.

On a soul level the life energy exchange in bullying, rape, killing, abuse or stealing is literal. The effect of intentional harm is to actually take power from another to use for oneself.

Through a process called power retrieval, we can gather the life energy that was stolen and return it to the victim. Power retrieval is extremely transformative. Both Rachel and Jose had power stolen from them by their attackers.

Most perpetrators are extremely unconscious of the damage they cause energetically. In fact, in the power exchange process, it is common for the higher self of the abuser to be very remorseful and for their own abuse experience to be revealed.

People steal life energy for many reasons. Most commonly, people steal life energy because they are disempowered themselves. They are compelled by their own powerlessness to feed on the soul substance of others. Some are completely self-centered and unaware of the harm their selfish behavior creates. Others may steal life energy because they are greedy or addicted to the rush of power and negative energy of abuse. Still others are so attached to the benefits they get at the expense of others that they deny any responsibility for their harmful actions. There is a spiritual principle that harming others absolutely harms the perpetrator because on the level of ultimate reality we are all connected.

Calling abusers into integrity by taking back what does not belong to them is an act of courage, but also of compassion. Supporting intentional harm, even unconsciously, harms everyone, while power exchange provides a healing opportunity for all involved.

Some people may end up in a victim position over and over. This is rarely coincidental and suggests an unconscious aversion to taking responsibility for their own life energy or a need to blame others for their life circumstances. In this case we are talking about volunteers rather than victims. This is not a statement of blame, as no one volunteers for suffering or abuse consciously.

We all have dysfunction in how we move through life. We each have incredibly complex systems to manage our life energy within ourselves and with other people. Discovering and taking responsibility for our patterns is the work. Ultimately, nothing happens in our psychic space without our permission. Whether we carry patterns of abuser, victim, or a mix of both, there is much that can be done.

## Power Retrieval Process

In *Allies & Demons* power or life energy is considered to be something real and concrete. Power can be lost in many ways; it may be given away in relationship, stolen by violence, bullying or abuse or drained off by chronic illness, neglect, grief, loss or long-term stress. Power may be lost through accident, surgery, birth trauma or by experiencing or witnessing a distressing event.

The good news is that personal power can also be retrieved, restored, returned and regained. Using the expertise of spirit guides who are skilled in working with power in this way, we can reclaim our own life energy and find resources and renewal in profound ways.

Personal power loss through trauma, abuse and neglect usually goes unrecognized and untreated by standard psychological protocols. Power loss can contribute to sleep issues, fatigue, apathy, low immune function, learning disabilities, anxiety, depression and autoimmune disorders to name a few. Regardless of the way the life energy was lost, the following processes can help restore us to wholeness.

In the guided inner journeys accompanying this chapter we will explore two approaches to power retrieval. The first is a process for Reclaiming Lost Power. To begin, we will connect with a guide who is skilled in working with energy, specifically in the gathering and restoring of lost soul force or personal power. This power retrieval guide will gather life energy we have lost through our lifetime that wants to be returned to us now.

This power reclamation may be done repeatedly and is very effective for power loss due to trauma, chronic abuse and neglect. Reclaiming Lost Power is also important for any power loss that was situational rather than perpetrated by an individual. For example, an accident, surgery, birth trauma, witnessing a distressing event, experiencing war or danger, moving, divorce, grief and loss, major disappointment can all result in power loss.

The second approach is the Inner Journey For Personal Power Retrieval & Exchange to restore life energy taken, received or stolen by a particular person or group of people. In this personal power retrieval process, we call in the higher self of the person who took our life energy with the help of our power retrieval guide and quite simply ask for our energy back.

Everyone has a higher self. The higher self in this context is the soul substance which resonates or is connected with the Universal Life Force. From a Christian standpoint, the higher self is the indwelling Christ consciousness. To the Buddhist, it is their Buddha nature. From a secular perspective, the higher self is the pure life force underlying the personality self.

It is profoundly healing and empowering to take back the life energy we have lost through trauma, abuse, neglect or unhealthy relationships. The Inner Journey For Personal Power Retrieval & Exchange is a clear path to restoring ourselves to spiritual, mental, emotional and energetic wholeness.

People often speak about giving their power away. In *Allies & Demons* we take this concept literally. Knowingly or unknowingly, we often give our power to others in relationships, in family systems, in power dynamics at work, school or social settings. This is most dramatic for those who have experienced trauma, abuse or neglect at the hands of an abuser or perpetrator.

Most perpetrators of violence, bullying or abuse of power are blind to the energetic reality that underlies their behavior. The energetic reality is that one of the main drivers for those who abuse others is power-seeking. Abusers and perpetrators usually have power loss or imbalance themselves and seek to empower themselves by stealing the life energy of others to make up for their own deficits.

Although power can be effectively stolen through acts of physical, sexual, emotional, political and social violence, the stolen energy cannot actually be used by the perpetrator in a healthy way. Like a blood transfusion requires matching blood types for integration, the life energy of others can never take the place of our own. Each of us must manage our own power to be fully functioning.

Those who try to empower themselves by using the life energy of other people are like energetic vampires, doomed to suck the soul substance of others in the dark, unable to tolerate the light of their own truth.

As mentioned in Chapter 7, it was important for Jose to take back the power that had been stolen from him by his attackers and for Rachel to retrieve the life energy she lost during the date rape.

In the personal power retrieval for Jose, we called in the higher self forms of the men who had attacked him. As aforementioned, everyone has a higher self and when called in this way they have to come. The three men each had a different relationship with the harm they had done Jose. Two of them apologized. One of them remained blank and quiet, though all of them were very willing to give back the power they had taken.

Jose's power exchange guide was a butterfly. Butterfly put her tube like proboscis tongue into the attackers chests and withdrew Jose's lost life energy as white and blue light. Butterfly then flew to Jose and transmitted this light into the top of his head.

Like a mosquito deposits its saliva as it siphons blood, the muggers had deposited shame, hatred and fear into Jose during the attack. Butterfly extracted this destructive energy from Jose and returned it to the men for them to manage in their own way.

Though it may never show on the surface, perpetrators suffer in their own particular way. In Rachel's personal power retrieval process, when she called the higher self of the boy who had raped her into her sacred place in non-ordinary reality, he appeared as an adolescent boy. At the time of the rape, the young man was 17, but his higher self was closer to 12.

The boy felt terrible for what he had done and wept with regret and shame. He showed Rachel that he had been beaten as a child and had transferred his rage and pain onto her during the rape. He reached into his stomach and offered her a golden ball of light, all of the innocence, hope and curiosity that he had taken. The light flowed across the space between them and into Rachel's heart and nervous system.

She told him that she forgave him and he dropped to his knees. She, too, began to cry as she returned the rage and pain that she had carried since that night on the beach. The boy took the ball of energy into his hands and a dog appeared, apparently his power animal, and helped him leave the scene.

Rachel was surprised at her willingness to forgive this person that she had feared and hated for so long, but it felt natural at the time. Upon reflection, she felt the healing power of forgiveness as a gift that she was giving herself rather than something she bestowed upon her attacker.

If you think that you may have stolen or gathered life energy from others, it's as important to give back what does not belong to you as it is to regain what has been lost. The process for giving back the life energy of others will be provided in the Inner Journey For Personal Power Retrieval & Exchange accompanying this chapter.

## Codependency & Managing The Life Energy Of Others

Not all power exchange between people is violent or intentionally abusive. It is common for lovers, friends, family and co-workers to attempt to help each other by taking on or carrying the problems, pain, responsibility or life energy of their counterpart.

When a child, partner or elder needs help in caring for themselves or their life situation, it is imperative for a stronger, more capable person to provide assistance. Caregiving for the young, the elderly, the sick or dying is a healthy, supportive act.

In relationships of all kinds, it is common for a more capable person to unconsciously agree to take on the life responsibilities of a less capable person. I use the word agree, because I believe the dynamics of all relationships are a series of agreements that we can renegotiate at any time.

Ultimately we are all responsible for our own life energy. When we try to avoid our personal growth work by abdicating our inner responsibilities to someone else, or try to "help" another by managing their problems for them, we are actually harming them on a soul level. The harm in taking too much responsibility for others or not owning our own power, is that we perpetuate a dysfunctional system of avoidance, fear and disempowerment.

This is one way to understand the concept of codependency. In codependency, each person is dependent upon the other for wholeness. Again, there are places where this is appropriate, like caring for an aging parent or helping a friend in a difficult life situation. But when wholeness in relationship depends upon filling in each other's gaps, then the gaps are perpetually reinforced and healthy personal growth is gridlocked. Sooner or later each person in a codependent relationship deteriorates because their life energy is being sourced through the human counterpart rather than from the Universal Life Source from which we all draw.

We must be very mindful of our motives when we want to "help" others by giving from our own life energy. Our personal resources of time, emotional attention, energy, money or material support are precious. We need to be conscious and mindful of our motives in giving, especially if we feel depleted or resentful in any way after doing for others.

Are we buying love, security or worthiness with our service? Are we feeding our ego narrative of ourselves as a martyr, sage or savior?

Are we robbing the person we intend to help of the opportunities for growth and self-esteem that natural consequence to their action or inaction provides? Are we avoiding our own needs, problems or personal growth work by focusing too much on the needs of others?

Conversely, we must be mindful when we need the help of others. Are we using our dependency as a way to avoid facing our fears and responsibilities? Do we collapse or dump our personal power as a way to manipulate others and trade adult love and equality in exchange for neediness, pity and perpetually being rescued?

As we've discussed, life energy in *Allies & Demons* has substance and form. When we try to carry the responsibilities or life energy of others, it weighs us down and keeps both parties unwhole. When we give away or lose our personal power to others in unhealthy ways, it can create devastating deficits for us as well.

It must be acknowledged that we are constantly exchanging life energy through our interactions with other people in a natural, healthy way. In work, home and daily life we converse, emote, have sex and interact through physical, mental, emotional, spiritual and energetic contact all the time. Learning about our own functional and dysfunctional patterns of energy management is crucial to maturity and balance in life.

We can give back that which does not belong to us and take back what is ours. There is a simplicity and freedom in taking care of our own side of the street and allowing others to do the same. Taking the Inner Journey For Personal Power Retrieval & Exchange can be an important part of that healthy balance.

## Neglect & Abandonment

Neglect is a particularly confusing form of trauma in that we are wounded by what did *not* happen. If we are beaten, molested or shamed, the abuse is obvious. However, if no one is ever home to feed us dinner, if we are not hugged or told we are loved, or if our emotional, mental, intellectual or spiritual needs go unmet, we are left with holes in our psyche that ache to be filled. Neglect is an ongoing or chronic experience of being uncared for.

Abandonment is when primary caregivers of a child are physically, mentally or emotionally unavailable or removed permanently either by leaving or death. Abandonment can be a one time event, a series of episodes or a chronic experience that leaves a legacy of insecurity, internal imbalance and unmet needs.

Young children cannot provide for themselves and being abandoned or uncared for by a caregiver means that they may not get the food, shelter or bonding experiences needed to stay healthy and alive. Abandonment is terrifying for children because they are powerless to advocate for themselves or to change their life circumstances in a substantial way.

Abandonment is a hot word in therapy and is frequently used to describe a trauma response in intimate relationships. Adults can be left or rejected, but adults cannot be abandoned. Abandonment is a life-threatening situation from the child's point of view and feeling abandoned in childhood can certainly create trauma. Adults may feel abandoned, but this is usually a triggering of an unresolved wound from a childhood experience. Adults have power to make choices and take constructive actions that unaided children do not.

Abandonment usually happens under the age of 12. The younger a person is when they are abandoned, the deeper the wound. Infants can experience abandonment at or after birth if they need to be hospitalized, separated from the mother or are given up for adoption.

There are myriad reasons that caregivers may not be able to adequately care for the children in their lives. Most commonly, the parents themselves were neglected and don't have the knowledge or skills to meet their children's needs.

When core needs go unmet, the psyche may attempt to compensate for what is missing in a variety of ways. For example, a person who is emotionally neglected may turn to food, drugs, alcohol or sex as a source of comfort and self-soothing. If a child is abandoned by a parent, they may decide to become self-sufficient and need nothing from anyone or conversely, they might become incapable of self-care and pull others in to care for them.

Like fingerprints, each person has their own unique strategy for dealing with unmet needs. Most presenting problems like addictions, anxiety, depression and financial or relationship issues can be viewed as misguided attempts to meet these core needs. If we can determine the authentic need and fill it, then the secondary issue will usually dissolve.

Both the soul retrieval process from Chapters 6 and 7 and power retrieval practices from this chapter are extremely effective in treating the often devastating effects of neglect and abandonment. By connecting with the unconditional love and compassion of our spiritual allies and developing an internal relationship of care and support as our own healthy self-parent, we are empowered to meet our authentic needs in present time.

## Wanda's Story

Wanda's mother was mentally ill. She never knew her father. The house was often dark because the electricity was shut off and they would run extension cords into the neighbor's yard for power to plug things in. Wanda learned how to shop with food stamps at a very young age. She did her best to take care of her younger sister and make sure they were fed and bathed.

Surprisingly, Wanda did well in school and made sure she and her sister were on time. They moved frequently, but Wanda was able to graduate from high school. She got a maintenance job for her town's public works department and eventually saved enough money to buy her own house. Though Wanda was high functioning in many ways, she had continued to care physically and financially for her sister and mother.

Wanda was bulimic and unable to maintain an intimate relationship. Through a series of inner child work sessions, we were able to retrieve many parts of Wanda who had been deeply neglected in the dark years of her childhood.

In the soul retrieval process for healing trauma, we found Wanda as a young girl, hungry and frightened. Adult Wanda felt tremendous love and respect for this girl and brought her to a riverside, her sacred place in non-ordinary reality.

Wanda's child self was depleted from chronic fear and neglect and her guides did a power reclamation process which was intense. Her life energy presented itself as tiny jewels that were gathered and returned to her. As we re-integrated the lost energy and reconnected with this child part, Wanda felt as if she were viewing the world with new eyes.

"I feel like colors are more vivid and sounds are clearer. My sense of smell is more intense," reported Wanda. Because of her natural tendency to be responsible in caregiving, she was able to develop strong and healthy self-parenting skills with herself.

When we explored Wanda's bulimia, she discovered what felt like an energetic backpack that she carried with her constantly. It was heavy, uncomfortable, and binging and purging on food was her attempt at emptying it out.

As we looked deeper, this energetic backpack was filled with the suffering and life energy of her mother and her sister. As a child, Wanda had hoped that if she was able to care enough for others, she might be cared for herself. She felt that she was strong enough to manage hard feelings that her mother was not and attempted to care for her mother by taking on the feelings that her mother was unable to take responsibility for.

Through a series of personal power retrievals, Wanda was able to empty the backpack and return the life energy she had taken on from her family and lovers. Her bulimia lessened and Wanda created healthier boundaries with her mother and sister.

## Sexual Abuse

It is estimated that 1 in 10 children will be sexually abused before their 18th birthday. Sexuality is connected to every aspect of our being as a creative life force. Because we live in a culture which is both obsessed with sex and unable to talk about it in a healthy way, sexual abuse can be disastrous for our sense of self and our relationships with others.

The work of *Allies & Demons* can bring tremendous healing and a new, positive sense of self to sexual abuse survivors. The inner journeys for soul and power retrieval provide potent, transformative tools for working through the many layers of harm and confusion resulting from sexual trauma and power loss.

Soul retrieval brings us to inner wholeness, self-compassion and love, by connecting us with the wounded, confused and often dissociated parts of ourselves. Again, this work is not about re-experiencing trauma, it is about bringing traumatized parts of the self out of trauma and into present time where they can recover and receive what they really need.

The power loss in sexual abuse is profound and confusing because the dynamics in sexual abuse are so complex. Unlike verbal or physical abuse, the experience of sexual abuse often includes emotional closeness and pleasurable sensation that is wrapped in betrayal, power stealing and selfishness. Survivors of sexual abuse often feel complicit or responsible for the experience, as perpetrators frequently deny or displace blame for their abusive behavior on the victims themselves.

Power retrieval restores important life energy to survivors, energy that brings a sense of wholeness, strength and empowerment vital to health and wholeness.

For example, Brandy worked as a stripper at a nightclub and made money as a sex worker on her off days. She had no interest in changing careers, but was plagued by anxiety and struggled with bouts of rage when interacting with a certain type of client. Brandy was taking a variety of medications, which she wanted to reduce because she didn't like how they made her feel.

As a child, Brandy and her mother lived communally in a large house with many residents coming and going. Her mother had a constant stream of lovers and Brandy often had to find another place to sleep. Between the ages of five and twelve, Brandy was sexually abused by a variety of nameless men, including many of her mother's lovers. At thirteen, Brandy was big enough and confident enough to say no to unwanted advances and the abuse stopped.

We did a series of soul retrievals to reconnect with the child aspects of Brandy and she developed a sense of love and care for herself. However, it was the series of power retrievals that were most important for her.

With the help of her guides and teachers, we went back to each of the men she could remember and took back the sexual, emotional, spiritual and energetic power they had taken from her. This work took place over a period of months and at the end of our work together, Brandy reported that both her anger and her anxiety were manageable and she reduced her medication.

In our last session, Brandy was thinking about going to school to become an esthetician. She considered her work in the sex industry as part of her healing and taking her power back - because she was in charge of who touched her and when. Rather than stealing Brandy's life energy, her clients paid her and now, through the power retrieval process, she felt more in charge of her life than ever before.

Although recovery from sexual trauma can be empowering and restorative, we each have our own internal timing and process that must be honored and trusted.

George, a thin, bookish college student, was referred to me through his talk therapist. They had been working together for a few years around what George felt was sexual abuse by his mother. As a child she often called George into her bed and he knew he felt "icky" about what happened there, but he had no clear memories of the abuse.

"I want to know what happened," said George. "Can we recover my memories using hypnosis?"

We worked through the first few inner journeys to ground George in aspects of his own higher self, which presented as a golden light radiating from his core and a large, kind sea turtle. However, when we tried to connect with his younger self, we came to a blank space filled with fog. It was warm and comfortable in the fog and George's turtle sat quietly there with him. The golden radiance suggested that we go no further, and in fact, try as we might over the next few sessions, we never moved past that pleasant foggy place.

George was disappointed, but I pointed out to him that the psyche has its own innate wisdom and that trusting our own inner timing is key for personal growth. Memories will reveal themselves when the time and circumstances are appropriate and healing can occur.

Often people will go years or even decades with no memories of their abuse or trauma. We may suddenly experience dreams, flashbacks or anxieties when our life becomes stable, when we begin addiction rehabilitation or other inner work.

Life gives us many opportunities for growth and healing. It is not uncommon for parents of young children to have their own trauma come up when their children reach the age they were when they were abused. Whatever the timing, it is important to trust the process of our own healing and not push too hard. There is a natural unfolding for recovery from sexual abuse that can and should be trusted.

## Spiritual Harm

Most people are familiar with the idea of emotional, mental or physical abuse. Spiritual abuse is a particularly devastating dynamic that separates the person from God, the Universal Life Force and their own authentic self.

The effects of spiritual abuse are hopelessness, despair, powerlessness, and a deep sense of existential isolation and loneliness. To some extent, all of us suffer from spiritual disconnection and lack of access to the true nature of reality simply in being human and living in the middle world.

There are basically two forces at work in the human realm - love and fear. Our existence on this plane of reality is a complex mixture of separation and connection. On the deepest level we are all part of a great whole, with love as the fundamental truth.

Once we enter the material plane, where everything is impermanent, our birth and death add a confusing or even terrifying element. On some level we know there is a greater reality, but human life separates us from it almost constantly, it seems. This separation is the root of our fear.

On a soul level, there is no birth and no death, but most of us don't live on a soul level. We turn to religious or spiritual teachings to guide us back to that ultimate truth of the eternal connection and oneness that underlies all things.

However, all light casts a shadow. Nearly every religion or spiritual tradition holds aspects of genuine truth. Unfortunately, human fear, misunderstanding and desire for power can twist these truths until they are nearly unrecognizable. When faith is twisted into fear, unconditional love may become judgment. Forgiveness becomes hatred of those who are different. The forces of creativity and sexuality are rejected, demonized and misunderstood.

We have struggled with the nature of our existence in human form since the beginning. Each culture has its own creation myths, spiritual traditions and wisdom stories to explain this human condition of seeming separateness from each other and from God. Truly understanding the cycles of birth and death is beyond the capacity of the egoic mind. Ultimately we are called to trust and surrender to the Infinite Wisdom of which we are all a part.

Our struggle to understand and make sense of what it means to be human is imperfect at best. The creation myth central to the Western world is the story of Adam and Eve. Other cultures have widely varied creation myths that try to make sense out of the existential separation we experience as humans and the cycles of birth and death.

In The Old Testament of the Bible, we are told that Eve and Adam eating from the tree of the knowledge of good and evil got us thrown out of Eden. The temptation or the desire to be God-like was our downfall. A fearful and angry god rejected us for our curiosity and disobedience.

There are so many ways to understand this story. Taken literally, it is the basis for centuries of misogyny and the disempowerment of women. It fosters a belief in a petulant and reactive deity and suggests that the separation we feel from Divine Presence is somehow punishment for original sin.

The tree of the knowledge of good and evil is our experience of duality in all its many forms - birth and death, male and female, day and night, love and fear. I don't claim to understand why it is so challenging to experience the true nature of reality and our ultimate connection with the Ground of Being. In fact, someday I hope to speak to The Manager about this issue.

In the meantime, many of us in the Western world were raised with the idea that the separation we experience as humans is our own fault, that we are basically unworthy of divine love and under the dominion of a punishing God.

## Spiritual Abuse

Steven was raised in a very conservative Christian family. He was a shy, creative youngest child with two older brothers. Dad worked and mom stayed at home. Steven's mom was an anxious woman who was very active in her church. The house was always spotless. The children were always neatly dressed. Dinner was on the table every night.

Frequently, Steven and his siblings were reminded that God would punish them for anything they did outside the narrow lines of mother's comfort zone. These threats from God were often followed by being hit or screamed at by Dad.

Discussion of anything sexual was forbidden and thought of as disgusting and sinful. Though the family went to church every week, Sundays were often a terrible day of fighting and verbal threats or abuse. When Steven's older brothers moved out of the house, Steven became the recipient of mother's anxiety and religious obsession.

Approaching high school, Steven began to feel attraction to boys, which was frightening and confusing for him. A handsome young man, he found it easy to date girls.

In college his sexual confusion increased and he began to use drugs and alcohol more and spend less time with people. His isolation and inner torment drove him to attempt suicide.

Steven took a handful of pills one night and hoped not to wake up. When he did wake up the next day, terribly sick, he just felt an extra layer of shame for having gone against God's word in attempting to die.

Intellectually, he knew that it was fine to be bisexual. He had gay and bi friends. However, spiritually and emotionally he was full of fear and confusion. None of this was spoken to anyone.

After college, Steven moved to San Francisco where he could pursue a more open lifestyle, but his anxiety and self-loathing got in the way. He felt that the universe was a harsh and unfriendly place, although he was naturally a very curious and spiritual person. He came to hate the word God and the punishment and judgment that his parents' views held for him. He felt hopeless.

Steven came to *Allies & Demons* sessions to work with his anxiety and depression. He wanted to try dating men, but couldn't gather the courage to put himself in the dating scene. The underlying message from his family was that being sexual in any way was lust of the flesh and that same gender sex was a mortal sin. A major part of Steven's identity, his sexuality, was seen as fundamentally wrong in the eyes of his parents and their conception of God.

Steven had internalized his parents' homophobia and lived in terrible conflict. His choices were - be true to his own nature and desires or follow the ideals of his parents' religion which forced a suppression of his authentic self. This is spiritual abuse.

Spiritual abuse is justifying any physical, mental, emotional, social, sexual, or financial harm as being required by God or an organization. This includes the misuse of religion or spirituality for the selfish, secular, or ideological ends of a leader, group or institution.

## All Light Casts A Shadow

All humans are fallible and imperfect, including religious and spiritual leaders. Once in a position of power and prestige, it is easy to want to justify or rationalize our own dysfunction so that we can stay in power and not have to do our own humbling work.

Religious and spiritual seekers often want their leaders to be superhuman, which supports the denial of wrongdoing. This is tragically obvious in the sexual abuse scandals of the Roman Catholic Church.

The tragedy of spiritual abuse is that selfishness, fear, pride and a need for control mask themselves as being Divine Will. Often bad behavior is justified as being in the service of God, the highest good of the individual or the group itself. This is darkness pretending to be light and it is the root of spiritual abuse. Any religion, institution, organization or teacher who claims to be perfect is dangerous because we live in a world of duality. There is no light that does not cast a shadow. We need to always be aware of this in ourselves and in others. Hoping to find perfection in any area of our life is a trap which sets us up to perpetrate or be victims of abuse. As long as we are human, it is important to know that perfection does not exist within the self or in our leaders.

It can be tricky to separate true teachings from false as they are often twisted up together. Once we have experienced spiritual abuse or confused false teachings as real, there is a tendency to withdraw from spirituality altogether rather than risk further harm.

People who use spiritual teachings to further their own selfish ends could be called false gods. If they do not claim to be gods themselves, they may point to a false god to legitimize their own destructive ends. False gods do not encourage our authentic self. They encourage followers to fit into their approved model of spirituality, however oppressive.

A terrible example of this is the radical Imams who incite the use of desperate young people as suicide bombers in the name of their god, to the horror of most practicing Muslims. Charismatic leaders like Jim Jones can initiate hundreds of people to mass suicide. The followers of Charles Manson believed that he was Christ and committed murder at his suggestion. Some religious cults, like the Branch Davidians, may require members to give everything they earn and turn over all property to the organization. Protestant white supremacist Ku Klux Klan members burn crosses on people's lawns and lynch lawful citizens. Satanic cults have been known to proscribe ritual physical and sexual abuse on adults and minors.

When a person's authentic self is rejected, demonized or dismissed because of religious or spiritual beliefs, that is spiritual abuse. When a religious or spiritual leader or group requires followers to do, feel or believe things that are counter to the highest good of the person, this is spiritual abuse. When guilt, shame, fear or punishment are threatened by some god as a way to control or manipulate individuals or groups, this is spiritual abuse.

For Steven, turning away from religion was part of his healing. There is a saying that religion is for those who are afraid of hell and spirituality is for people who have already been there.

Steven now has a natural distrust of anything named as religious, but finds a deep sense of connection in nature and through his art, photography and music. Through a series of soul and power retrievals, Steven was able to release the guilt and shame around his sexuality, to separate his own reality from his parents' beliefs and find the courage to start dating men. His anxiety and depression have eased and he feels hopeful about his future.

## Hope

Although it takes time and perseverance, healing trauma, abuse and neglect is some of the most rewarding and transformative work one can do. The wounds from our life may show their face over and over, but never in the same way if we're willing to work with them directly. Recurrences of trauma or triggering of unresolved emotional issues are an opportunity to grow. The hope and healing that's available is life changing.

# *Taking The Inner Journeys For Power Retrieval*

There are two inner journeys for power retrieval: *Reclaiming Lost Power* and the *Inner Journey For Personal Power Retrieval & Exchange*. *Reclaiming Lost Power* is effective for restoring life energy lost through accidents, illness, addiction, trauma, grief, neglect and abandonment.

The *Inner Journey For Personal Power Retrieval & Exchange* is essential for healing abuse or trauma perpetrated by an individual or group. This journey is also effective for recalibrating codependent patterns and healing or severing dysfunctional relationships. If you have taken the life energy of others, knowingly or unknowingly, this journey provides a powerful opportunity for healing and reparations by helping you return life energy you may be holding that does not belong to you.

These journeys may be done repeatedly to reclaim energy lost in past or present time. Some practitioners make power retrieval a weekly practice for renewal and regeneration for general energy loss in daily life.

> *Guided audio for the two inner journeys for power retrieval is available at www.reneemckenna.com.*

## *Make yourself comfortable and become aware of your body...*

*Take a few deep breaths and open your inner senses. Call in the guides and allies you have connected with previous journeys. And notice where they are in relation to you.*

*Hold the intention that we are going to reclaim lost power. Reclaiming and restoring lost life energy is important to be fully functioning. Your allies are going to help restore your life energy using an ancient healing practice called power retrieval. You don't need to understand what this means. The process is unique to each person. You just need to be open and observe.*

*Ask your allies to show you a place in nature where we can do a power retrieval. This may be a place you've been before or it may be someplace new. Once you are in this place, notice what's around you. When you are ready, ask for a guide or teacher who can assist with power retrieval. It may be one of the allies you've already worked with or it may be something new. See what comes. It doesn't have to make any sense.*

*Notice what the form of the power retrieval guide is. What is their character like? Are they willing to help you now? Where are the guides in relation to you? They may create an energetic configuration around you that will help with power retrieval. Just be present and observe.*

*Ask this power retrieval guide to gather the life energy that was lost or drained away during neglect, abuse or trauma in your life. Notice what the guide or teacher does.*

*In* Allies & Demons, *all time is present time. Guides and teachers work in the energetic or spiritual realm and they can gather lost life energy and bring it back to you. You may be able to track them as they go back across space and time to gather this life energy or you may not. If you are able to track them, notice what happens as they gather up the life energy you've lost. They may go back to the places where life energy was lost or they may gather it in a different way.*

*Does this energy have a form? A color? A density? What is the process they use to gather your life energy? When the guide is finished, they will return to you and pour the power they have gathered into your body/mind/energy system. Notice where the energy pours into your body. Does it enter through the top of your head? Your forehead? Your heart or belly? How does the guide return your life energy to you now? How do you sense, feel or imagine this happening?*

*Assist by breathing the energy in. Open to receive this life energy back on all levels; physically, mentally, emotionally, spiritually, sexually, socially, energetically. Integrating this energy all the way down to the soles of your feet, out to the tips of your fingers and up to the crown of your head. You might feel a filling sensation or you might not. Take all the time you need to reclaim your life energy. This is a restorative, renewing process.*

*When that feels complete, ask your guides and teachers if anything wants to be done or communicated to be complete with this for now. Thank your allies for their help.*

*Feel free to write about your experience in your journal.*

## Personal Power Retrieval & Exchange

This Journey For Personal Power Retrieval & Exchange is essential for healing trauma or abuse perpetrated by an individual. This session is also an opportunity to return the life energy of others that we may have taken on knowingly or unknowingly.

## *Take a few long, slow breaths to relax the body and become more present...*

*Call in your guides and teachers from previous journeys, any allies you've connected with or any aspects of your own highest self or elements of nature. We are calling in spiritual help. Viscerally feel where these spiritual allies are in relation to you. Are they beside you, behind you, in front of you? Where do you experience them in the room right now?*

*Bring to mind the person you will retrieve or exchange power with. Your allies will do the work, but it is helpful to have a clear intention. Where have you been disempowered? Where have you disempowered others? Pick a situation or relationship. If there is a trauma, bring that situation into mind. If there was a particular person perpetrating abuse or neglect, bring that person into mind. If there's a particular person who may have knowingly or unknowingly stolen your life energy, we can reclaim it from them now. If you have abused or harmed someone, we will be returning power to them in this process.*

*Once you have your intention, ask your guides and teachers to show you where the power retrieval or exchange should happen. Sense, feel or imagine a path or stairway that leads to a place in nature where we can do this power retrieval. This may be a place you've been before, or it may be someplace new. Notice what the path or stairs are made of. What's the quality of the air, the light? Follow this path or stairs that leads to a beautiful and powerful place where we can do a power re-*

*trieval and exchange. Trust what comes, be curious about what presents itself and go with it.*

*Notice where your guides are in relation to you in this place. They may create an energetic configuration around you that will help with power retrieval.*

*Call in your power retrieval guide from the last inner journey and ask if any of your other guides and teachers will assist with this personal power retrieval. If you do not have a power retrieval guide, ask for one now and see what comes. Notice the form of your power retrieval guide and where they are in relation to you.*

*Recall your intention for this process. Bring to mind the person you will retrieve or exchange energy with. Call that person's highest self into the sacred place. Ask your allies to help. Everyone has a higher self and when called in this way, they have to come, they have no choice. They may come escorted by their own guides and teachers.*

*Notice what or who comes. The higher self of a person is an aspect of their soul energy that they may or may not have access to in ordinary reality.*

*Once the higher self of the person is present, ask their higher self if they know why they are here. Are they aware that they are holding your life energy? Once we become consciously aware of the dynamic of personal power loss, no one can keep our life energy from us when we decide we want it back. We are here to receive that which was taken or what we gave to them, knowingly or unknowingly. They have no choice but to give it back because it doesn't belong to them. Lying is not allowed on this plane of reality. They have to stay in integrity. They have no choice.*

*Notice if there is anything that wants to be done or communicated between you and this person. When you are ready, tell them that you want your life energy back. Use whatever words feel most true for you. The person may have stolen this energy, taken it without knowing or you may have given it to them.*

*Ask your guides and teachers to be intercessors to get your life energy back from the person who took it. Notice how your power retrieval guide gathers your personal power from this person and returns it to you now. Does it have a color, light or sound? How does it enter your body? Open to receive this life energy on all levels and into all systems of your body.*

*When the power retrieval feels complete, ask your allies if anything else wants to be done. Notice if there is anything that this person wants to communicate to you regarding this energy exchange.*

*Check within yourself to see if you took anything on from this person. If you are unsure, ask your power retrieval guide if you are holding anything from this person. If you have taken the life energy of someone else, you will return it to them now.*

*If the other person is unable or unwilling to take their life energy back, then their guides and teachers will appear to receive it for them. Ask your allies how to release or let go of anything that doesn't belong to you.*

*Does this person's life energy have a form? How is it extracted from your body and energy system? How is the energy returned? Take all the time you need.*

*Ask if there is anything that wants to be done or communicated with you, with the higher self of the other person, or your guides and teachers. If that feels complete, then the higher self of the person you called in can be excused. When you are ready, return to follow the path or stairway that lead you here. Bring all of this into your body, remembering everything fully.*

*Write about your experience.*

CHAPTER 9

# Dissolving Depression

*Our deepest fear is not that we are inadequate.*
*Our deepest fear is that we are powerful beyond measure.*
*It is our light, not our darkness that most frightens us.*

— MARIANNNE WILLIAMSON

Working with depression in *Allies & Demons* is three-fold. First, we need to dissolve or unlock the depression itself. Second, we need to reclaim our authentic self that has been hidden in our consciousness. Third, we need to retrieve the power drained away by the depression.

Depression is an energetic configuration that has its own intention and life force to some extent. You might understand depression as a conglomeration of a person's emotional pain, as a behavior that's passed down along family lines, as a physical condition, or as a demon or entity that fills in the gaps where the authentic self should be. From the perspective of *Allies & Demons*, depression is a destructive and depleting energetic formation that can and should be extracted or dissolved.

The effect of depression can be taken literally, as the pressing down of the authentic self. There is a saying that depression is anger turned inward. For some, depression is a relentless, negative, hopeless, self-hating voice. For others it is a black cloud of numbness sucking all color and meaning out of life. Mild depression can make life dull, difficult and exhausting. Major depression can be debilitating and lead many to take their own life rather than continue in the dark chasm of suffering and despair.

According to the World Health Organization, 300 million people worldwide suffer from depression and it is the leading cause of disability on earth. My own experience with depression was like a thick, heavy blanket that covered my life. I would binge on food, throw it up, masturbate and then sleep and sleep and sleep, to wake up and start the cycle again.

In my darkest depression, I had a lot of outward success. I was doing well in school. I had a handsome boyfriend who made a lot of money. Our families expected us to get married. My physical needs were taken care of and my future looked good on paper.

When I was out in the world, I put on a happy face. Inside, however, I hated my life. I felt nothing but shame, guilt and resentment. I "should" be happy, I believed, but there seemed nothing to be happy about.

## Obligation

"Should" is the language of obligation. An obligation binds us morally, socially, relationally or professionally to act in ways that uphold the status quo. Obligation is an outside expectation directed at internal experience.

Obligation is a duty that we are bound to whether it serves the highest good or not. It generally fears change and blocks personal growth that challenges or undermines existing cultural or religious structures. Obligation is different than commitment, although from the outside they may appear very similar.

Optimally, commitment comes from a place of integrity, compassion, love and service. Commitment can provide security and accountability and create a container to evolve and work through difficulties we might run from otherwise. Commitment is voluntary and comes from within. Obligation is generally rooted in external expectation and there seems to be no choice.

Whenever I hear the word should, a little flag goes up for me. Who said you should? Why should you? Does the "should" serve the highest good of everyone involved including yourself? These are important questions to ask.

My own depression kept me in a life of obligation. Obligation to a boyfriend I no longer wanted to be with. Obligation to an idea of who I thought I should be, who my friends and family wanted me to be, even who my teachers wanted me to be.

I was completely separated from my own life energy, from my feelings, wants, dreams and desires. Separated from my essence, I had no hope. I felt like an animal with its leg caught in a claw trap, trying to chew the limb off to escape.

In hindsight, there were parts of myself that I felt could never and should never see the light of day, mostly my emotional and spiritual sides. From the perspective of my authentic self, I was living a lie. My life looked great on the outside, but it was a bleak pit on the inside.

I had a range of social masks and I simply couldn't tell the truth. I despised my life. I wanted to die. I believed that if people really knew me, they would hate me like I had come to hate myself. Telling the truth wasn't even an option, because the truth seemed so unreasonable and would cause so much trouble that I was willing to implode rather than risk bringing it out into the world.

I desperately wanted change and was equally terrified of it at the same time. I wanted to leave my relationship. I wanted to get away from my family. I wanted to change my body. I wished I felt, thought and looked differently. I wished I was dead.

Finally, it was the suffering of depression itself which drove me to the place where my fear of change was less than the suffering of staying where I was.

Ultimately, every experience in our life can lead us to higher good if we are open and willing. Pain and suffering can be part of the path. We don't have to suffer to evolve, but if we are unwilling to live from a place of our own truth, there will be consequences. Emotional, mental and even physical pain and illness all point to the need for change.

## Fear of Change

Tom was a good friend of mine. His mother Paula died of breast cancer at age 52, when Tom was 19. Paula was always depressed and though his parents stayed together, their relationship was terrible. Tom's dad was abusive and Paula lived a life of quiet desperation, obligated to take care of everyone but herself.

I asked Tom if he thought his parents should have divorced. "Absolutely," he said, "but Mom was a devoted Catholic and would rather have died of breast cancer than get divorced. In fact, I think she saw cancer as a way out without having to make any hard choices. She died three months after her diagnosis. She had no reason to live."

Though change can be scary and even feel destructive, the very nature of life is change. Often old structures need to fall so that new ones can take their place. When a tomato plant produces fruit and goes to seed, it is not a failure. It has completed its work and the dead stalk and leaves enrich the soil for new plants to come.

When a commitment becomes an obligation, it has lost its spirit. This is not to say that it is best to run away when things get difficult. Often great growth springs from moving through hardship. But we need to be aware of our motives. Fear of change is a terrible reason to do or not do something. Love and service to ourselves and others is solid ground to make decisions from.

Life is a verb, always changing and challenging us to grow. Discerning how to best participate in our own evolutionary process is the inner work we need to do.

Determining where we are being called to grow can be a complex process. The real work begins with gathering the courage, energy and resources needed to make and sustain positive change. There is always help available. This is where spiritual practice and spiritual help can be invaluable.

We live in an interactive universe. The Life Force is always offering help and guidance, if we learn to pay attention. Often this help comes through what many call grace.

## Conversations With God

Grace is another word for serendipity or coincidence. Grace is coincidence that has a heart. It can be understood as part of our conversation with the Universe. What we believe, the decisions we make, the actions we take can be seen as how we express ourselves to the Universe. Grace is how the Divine talks back.

For example, Alison's mother loved purple butterflies. After her mother passed away, Alison was depressed and grieved deeply. She missed her mother terribly. They had always loved shopping together and soon after her mother's death, Alison started seeing purple butterflies everywhere. Someone sent her a card with a purple butterfly on it. Purple butterflies seemed to land nearby when she was walking her dogs in the park. While shopping, she continually came across jackets, t-shirts and sweaters with purple butterflies. At the end of a remote work event, Alison and her co-workers were surprised with a visit to a butterfly sanctuary. It was filled with purple butterflies.

Alison had never been very religious or spiritual. However, over time, when she saw a purple butterfly, she felt a strong connection to her mom. Alison came to believe that the butterflies were a part of her mother's spirit, affirming their soul connection, a mark of grace.

I remember a day in my early 20's when I experienced grace in a clear and loving way. I had told my boyfriend at the time a deep secret. The secret was that I had questions about my own sexuality and sexual orientation. Talking about my sexuality was a risk at that time. This man acted out my worst fear. He freaked out and asked me to leave. I was devastated. I remember driving away, crying hysterically, feeling like there was no one safe to talk with. I went home still sobbing. I was surprised by a knock on my door soon after I arrived. I wiped my face and went to the door to find the one person in the world I had told my sexual secret to, a dear friend from college I hadn't seen in years.

"I was in town and thought I'd stop by and say hello," she said. Oh my Goodness. The perfect person at the perfect time. We had lunch and laughed and cried more. I felt so much better. That experience affirmed something I already knew - that God often works through people.

The universe is always communicating with us. We need to learn how to understand the language. I believe there is no problem without a solution and that there are hints and signs and symbols all around to point us toward the next right step in our life - if we pay attention.

Sometimes we resist the call to grow. First we get a memo and then we receive a letter, then a street sign, then a billboard and finally, if we don't pay attention, we get a gravestone. We can make choices all along the way, but we often don't have hope that things can change, so we ignore, turn down or just don't see the options, and we stay stuck.

Richard Bach, author of the iconic book *Jonathan Livingston Seagull* said, "We are never given a dream without also being given the power to make it come true."

We may have to work for it, however.

How we misunderstand the idea of spiritual help is illustrated in a story about a very religious pastor. There is a terrible flood in his town and everyone is being evacuated. The fire department's going door-to-door telling people to leave. They knock on the pastor's door and he tells them, "Oh I'm not worried. God's going to save me."

The water rises so high that firemen in boats rescue people out of second floor windows. The pastor waves the boat to keep going. "God's gonna save me," he says, and the boat passes by.

The water continues to rise and the pastor has to climb out on his roof. A helicopter comes by and drops down a rope ladder. "God's gonna save me," yells the pastor and the helicopter flies on.

The pastor finds himself at the pearly gates of Heaven and he asks St. Peter, "Why didn't God save me?" St. Peter replies, "We sent a fireman, a boat and a helicopter. What more do you want?"

## Disease Model Of Depression

The disease model of depression is misguided. Many people are told that depression is an illness, like diabetes. Doctors are trained to believe that once you have depression you will always have it, and the best you can do is just treat the symptoms and medicate yourself for the rest of your life. This is not my experience.

There are physical markers for depression like lowered serotonin levels, fatigue and sleep disturbance. The body and the brain are extremely elastic and work as a unit. Although modern science has given us amazing insights into the mind and body, one of the downsides of the scientific approach has been the compartmentalization of different aspects of human beings. The body, mind, emotions and spirit are often seen as separate systems, rather than as interactive parts of a whole. What happens in the body is reflected in the mind. What happens in the mind is reflected in the body. The good news is that making constructive changes in any of our systems can affect positive change in the body/mind/spirit complex as a whole.

If you don't do physical exercise, you will weaken. If you work out three times a week, no matter what age you are, your body will get stronger. This is true for the mind as well. Many studies show that using the brain keeps it in shape, just like push ups will tone your arms and chest.

Our spirit is perhaps the most flexible of all of our systems and the least exercised. Living in ways that are fulfilling, enriching, connecting and joy-producing creates incredible positive change in outlook, mood and feeling.

The physical aspects of depression are the body's expression of a systemic problem - the rejection, neglect or abandonment of the true self.

## The Dragon Of Depression

Working with depression is absolutely the hero's journey. We need to be willing to go into the cave, face down the dragon and bring back the treasure that has been hidden and hoarded for so long.

The advantage of working with the active imagination is that we can make non-physical beliefs, feelings and experiences concrete and work with them directly. The energy of depression is certainly palpable for anyone who has suffered with it. Through the journeys accompanying this chapter, our active imagination will give form and substance to the demon of depression itself. These journeys will enable us to transform the depression in powerful ways and retrieve valuable life energy that was drained away or lost.

There are lots of ways to understand the energy of depression. In *Allies & Demons* it's often a protective energetic formation which attempts to keep the authentic self from harm, often never letting it see the light of day. It's rooted in fear and hopelessness, born from the lie that who we really are has no place in the world and will never be supported. In fact, from the perspective of depression, expressing the true self is dangerous or even deadly.

It is deadly to express our true selves. But only deadly to the depression, because depression cannot live in the light of the true self. Depression is like a parasite that feeds on darkness, sadness, pain, and despair.

Our purpose is to find the authentic need that underlies the depression. With the help of our guides and teachers and our own compassion, we can fulfill the underlying authentic need. This is an alchemical process that transforms our demons into allies.

The *Dissolving The Demon Of Depression* process accompanying this chapter powerfully transforms the demon of depression into a helpful protector or dissipates it altogether. Once the energy of the depression has shifted, we can then begin the work of reclaiming and integrating the authentic self which underlies the depression. Reclaiming the part of our true nature which was lost to depression is like finding the treasure in our own hero's journey.

Depression can have many layers. This may be a multifaceted process of transforming darkness and retrieving light, of releasing lies and embracing the truth, of dissolving our fear and connecting with hope. As with many of the inner journeys in *Allies & Demons*, we may have to repeat these journeys to dissolve the many layers of depression that have built up over time.

## Transforming The Demon

The first step in working with depression is to look at the person's relationship to the depression itself. Nothing lives in our psychic space without our permission. Whether we're aware of it or not, at some point in our life, this depression has served us. Depression may serve us as a survival skill that keeps us small and safe, a way to avoid facing our fears, or as a way to press down or block our natural life flow.

It can be a jarring idea to consider that we have an attachment to something as difficult and damaging as depression. However, understanding what this relationship is and how it has served us can provide the key to unlocking its chains. Depression can easily become a part of someone's identity and their narrative of who they are as a person.

We will use a method to dissolve the depression similar to what we did in Chapter 5 when we worked with the inner critic. In this work, we address the demon of depression directly. We clarify what the underlying need driving the depression is, and bring spiritual and energetic healing directly to the energy of the depression itself. This either dissolves the depression completely or transforms it into a more helpful, protective form.

## Juliet's Story

I had been seeing Juliet for about six months. She was a tall, athletically built young woman, a stylish dresser who wore no makeup, and spoke three languages. She felt isolated and depressed since her boyfriend moved out of their apartment. We were working with the trauma she experienced after being in a terrible car accident as a teenager.

Juliet called me one day, deeply depressed. She had been in the house for three days and didn't feel like she could leave. Luckily, I was able to see her right away. She arrived at my office in tears.

Juliet described feeling numb and cut off from herself. She binge-watched TV because she couldn't sleep, and hadn't been able to attend her college classes. The narrative in her head was that she was worthless, lazy and unlovable. When we brought attention to the numbness in her body and the hateful voice in the left side of her head, we discovered a defensive structure that tried to protect her by keeping her safe at home.

One notable aspect of depression is that it seems to feed on suffering. Through the inner journey work found at www.reneemckenna.com, we can actually dialogue with the depression itself and gather important information about it.

When I asked Juliet if she could recall the first time she had this particular feeling of depression, she got the visual of herself in the hospital after the car crash that had nearly taken the life of one of her friends and left her with chronic back pain.

The depression was obviously holding her back from things she really wanted, like dating and doing her best in school. When we looked deeply into it, after the accident, the depression was a protective device to keep her safe. It kept her safe from taking risks, but at the expense of her overall wellbeing. She could see how this energy had been an attempt at self-protection, but it didn't serve her anymore. In fact, the depression was draining her power and keeping her from the full life she craved.

Once she became willing to consciously take the risks of dating and succeeding at school, she also became willing to let this depressive, protective configuration go. Interestingly, the depression had developed its own agenda and didn't want to be released. We were confronting her long-standing habit of isolation and retraction.

Luckily, habits of mind and body are just habits and can be replaced with healthier, more constructive actions. Through the process accompanying this chapter, we were able to release the depression and connect with the positive spiritual energy of her deceased grandmother, which she could draw on in times of need.

From my understanding, Juliet's depression shifted dramatically. We subsequently did a soul retrieval and a journey to reclaim lost power to complete her healing. Juliet graduated from her college program and was accepted to graduate school in another city just before she completed her work with me.

## Restoration

An important part of releasing depression is to heal the inner wounding that is often the genesis of our suffering using the soul retrieval method described in Ch. 7. Aristotle once said, "Nature abhors a vacuum," and that is true in the psyche as well. When the authentic self of the person is rejected, abandoned, neglected or traumatized, depression is one of the energetic formations that will arrive to fill the space.

When the energy of the depression is released, we then need to retrieve the soul energy of the authentic self which either fled or was de-pressed. In order for this reintegration to be effective, we need to be willing to love, support, and nourish the authentic self parts which have been absent, abused or neglected. We need to be willing to surrender to our own highest good, gather our own inner treasures and bring them into the world.

One of the ways to understand the fatigue and power loss that goes with depression is that it takes a tremendous amount of life energy to hold down the authentic self. In depression, a major portion of our personal power, whether we are aware of it or not, is being used to depress our life force below the level of consciousness.

I have a strong visual that goes with this - a person pushing or pressing a part of themselves down into a dark basement. Our true nature is always struggling to express itself in the world and it takes constant pressure to keep it at bay. This struggle depletes the depressed person so that they have no energy left to support their authentic self.

Frequently, depression is a protective device that shields us from putting ourselves out in the world in ways where we might risk failure, disapproval or rejection. Conversely, depression can also keep us from risking success, hope and fulfillment. Depression can help us bypass confronting things like going back to school, pursuing creative endeavors, leaving a dead relationship, changing careers, or otherwise pursuing our dreams and goals.

Most of us find our light, not our darkness, to be the most frightening thing.

Though we may have experienced complete powerlessness over the energy of depression previously, once the demon has been dissolved or transformed, our relationship with our own authentic self becomes central.

## Addie's Story

Addie was a bank manager in her late thirties. She had suffered with depression since she could remember and came to me shortly after leaving a job she hated. Addie was very sensitive and insightful, but was feeling lost and purposeless in her life.

Her depression was a terrible inner voice that told her she was worthless and stupid. She had attempted suicide the year before. The suicidal thoughts had returned and she was scared.

When we addressed the depression directly, it was like a large, angry man who hated her. As we looked more deeply, the depression revealed itself as a twisted attempt to manage difficult feelings.

Addie was the only child of mild-mannered Midwestern parents. Her father was a college professor. Her mother a bookkeeper. Growing up she remembers everyone reading a lot. No fighting. Not much intimate interaction of any kind really.

As a teenager, she recalls cutting herself. "I had all these really intense feelings and cutting my skin was a way to let the pressure out. I felt really ashamed of it, and only cut where it wouldn't be seen, but it actually made me feel better at the time."

Addie felt ashamed of her depression, too. "Nothing bad happened to me. I don't have any good reason to want to kill myself all the time. I just feel crazy."

Through the *Dissolving The Demon Of Depression* process, the terrible voice was extracted and a spiritual ally of a great whale took its place. Whale was wise, ancient, incredibly powerful and loving.

When we explored the origin of the depression, we came upon Addie as a very young child playing by herself. She was having deep feelings and didn't know what to do with them. We brought this intuitive, quietly passionate child to Whale. Whale validated Addie's emotional nature as a gift and benefit, not something to be hidden or ashamed about.

This soul retrieval connected Addie with the constructive, creative portal that her feelings could provide. Soon after, she began working on a short story she had always dreamed of writing. Eventually, she joined a writer's group, where her emotions served her artistry and her depression noticeably lifted.

Depression is like a complex prison for the self. Whatever part of us that's being pressed down or imprisoned, we need to rescue and reclaim. We need to be willing to create the structures, the environment and the power to be able to support this part of our authentic self in our lives and in the world. This might be inconvenient, difficult or even require a complete life makeover. But this is our work, to be in support of our true self. The alternative is a living death.

## Suicide Is A Bummer

We can't have an adequate discussion about depression without addressing the issue of suicide. Unfortunately, I have known many people who have taken their own life. There are myriad reasons people kill themselves. Generally suicide is an attempt to escape suffering. It is a permanent solution to a temporary problem.

Although wanting to escape pain is totally understandable, on a soul level suicide doesn't work as a way to relieve suffering. In fact, on a soul level, suicide can even complicate our problems by adding a layer of massive self-destruction on top of the difficulties already existing.

There are different ways to understand what happens to a soul after death, if one believes in the continuity of a soul at all. From the Buddhist perspective of karmic reincarnation, human life is a place to grow and evolve in higher truth. The laws of cause and effect which govern karma are inescapable. Thus, to commit suicide in this lifetime is an attempt to cheat karma rather than doing the inner work needed to heal.

In this light, it is better to do the work to heal here and now, otherwise it is likely that we will end up in similar circumstances until we get it right. Committing suicide, because of the exponential suffering it often causes others, technically can add extra baggage to a person's karmic patterns. Meaning that rather than relieving the person's burden by hitting the reset button of death, the person committing suicide may actually be making their own burden heavier.

## Shadow Keeper

Depression has many causes. The impetus for depression could be emotional, social, relational, spiritual or physical. If one has suffered major depression the effects can have lasting impact even after the depression has lifted.

For example, Hillary is perky, petite brunette in her late thirties who works as a research director in a large biotech firm. Hillary came to *Allies & Demons* sessions to work with strong feelings that were coming up as her daughter became depressed in her mid teens.

Over time, Hillary's own trauma surfaced. For five years, from age seventeen to twenty-two, Hillary had suffered with her own suicidal depression, a dark part of her life that she rarely spoke of. As a teen, Hillary had been hospitalized multiple times and attempted suicide twice. As happens to many parents, the age and experience of her child was bringing up her own unresolved pain so that it could be healed.

Using Hillary's active imagination, we were confronted with frightening and mysterious parts of herself that she had kept hidden away as best she could. We found part of her at eighteen in the police station, another in the hospital after taking a bottle of pills. In another inner journey we found a particularly hopeless and desperate part of her alone in her apartment at 4am, having just drunk bleach.

Using the inner journey for soul retrieval accompanying this chapter, we brought these disparate parts of herself, one by one, to her sacred place in nature, a warm, wooded hiking trail next to a stream. Long term depression can have similar effects to trauma in severing or shattering the self into many fragments over time. The powerful inner journeys of *Allies & Demons* may need to be repeated multiple times to recover, restore and reintegrate the many parts of the self damaged by the depressive experience.

Hillary's inner journeys uncovered some parts of herself that were nearly catatonic, unable to speak or move on their own. Her power animal, a loving cocker spaniel, was able to gently coax these depressed parts of her out of their past traumatic scenes and into her sacred place where they could rest and begin to heal in present time. Other parts of her were crazed with rage, guilt and embarrassment.

"I don't even recognize these parts of myself. I've felt so much shame about this time in my life. I don't understand what happened or why I did what I did. They are like shadow keepers. They hold all this darkness, all this pain, but there is power there, too. They almost killed me," Hillary observed, crying.

With the help of Hillary's power retrieval guide, an orb of white and multi-colored light with a comet like tail, we began to restore some of the life energy that was lost through the depression and suicide attempts. The orb went back to the apartment where she had tried to kill herself, collected her lost power and transmitted it into the chest of one of her devastated self parts. Color, awareness and vitality began to return. We repeated this inner journey over and over, gradually restoring her systems to full power in present time.

Every part of us holds valuable life energy. Over time Hillary came to see that she had rejected very powerful parts of herself that held anger, pain and fear - feelings which she was uncomfortable with.

"Intellectually I know that it's OK to be angry, but honestly, my anger scares me. It feels so ugly and out of control. I'm much more comfortable being sad or trying to be understanding rather than letting myself be mad."

Feelings are information and if we reject them, we disempower ourselves by dismissing or depressing the messages they offer. Anger can be particularly potent and complex. In its purest form, anger signals that our boundaries are being crossed or that something is out of integrity. Anger can provide energy and power to stand our ground or push back against injustice, manipulation or being treated poorly.

Suppressing healthy anger is like giving ourselves a death message on a soul level. A death message means that our needs are unimportant and we are unwilling or unable to care for our authentic self. Tragically, people may kill themselves rather than honor all of who they are.

The human psyche presents more like a crowd than like a single organism. Often the work of self part integration, of recovering from depression or trauma, is like setting a table and inviting long lost relatives into your home. We want to create a safe internal space, where all parts of ourself are welcome to gather so that we can get to know them over time. Developing a practice of compassion and curiosity about ourselves, even the painful parts, is immensely rewarding.

As Hillary came to understand and care for her shadow keepers, she was forced to confront her anger at her parents for being emotionally unavailable to her as a kid. She wanted to jump over the anger and just be compassionate to them, a very common dynamic called *spiritual bypass.*

Spiritual bypass is when we try to skip over the messy feelings like rage or fear and just go right to forgiveness and understanding or empathy. It is only by moving honestly through the digestive process of all of our emotions that we can absorb the nutrients of an experience and excrete the rest. If we try to avoid our authentic rage and fear, they just go underground and pop up like zombies trying to eat our brains. When we face, feel and move through our feelings, we grow and mature naturally.

As Hillary made room for her anger by working with the suicidal parts of herself, she had a profound realization.

"I read a study at work that blew me away. It was a massive study, over 1,000,000 women and girls by a Dr. Ojvind Lidegaard, of the University of Copenhagen in Denmark, about birth control pills, depression and suicide," Hillary explained. "They found that birth control pills double to triple the rate of depression, especially in teens. My depression started right after I went on the pill as a senior in high school and my depression ended a few weeks after I stopped taking birth control five years later. It's so intense. My depression was a chemical reaction to the hormones."

This realization deepened her forgiveness of herself for her suicide attempts. It also evoked another level of anger because she felt that on some level she knew that the depression was chemical and kept taking the birth control anyway.

"I think being depressed worked for me in a really negative way. That seems crazy, but depression kept me quiet and disempowered. It was easier to be depressed than to be all of who I am."

Over time Hillary made peace with her shadow keepers and shared with her daughter about her own painful past and how she identified with her daughter's times of despair. She became less afraid of her own rage and expressed gratitude at feeling more permission to be all of who she is, not just the "nice parts."

## Liam's Story

Liam is a lawyer who dreamed of being a musician. Liam's father was a lawyer, and Liam's grandfather was a lawyer. As a sophomore in college, Liam told his family that he wanted to change his major from pre-law to sound engineering. His father told him he would be welcome to do that, but he would need to pay for the rest of his college by himself. Liam finished law school, passed the bar exam and went to work in his father's law firm. He hated it, but he wanted to please his father.

When Liam came to see me he was incredibly depressed. He had moved into a new apartment six months before and had never unpacked the boxes. Although Liam worked in the same office as his father, they rarely saw each other and most of their communication went through Liam's mother, who he spoke with every day.

Liam's power animal was a wolf who lived in a wild and beautiful forest. As we explored Liam's depression and his authentic self, Liam experienced himself as being in a jail cell. His mother was the jailer and his father was the judge. Over time, Liam realized that the cell door was unlocked. He became very hopeful, his depression lifted. He began to go out at night to listen to music and made plans to go back to school.

With the help of Wolf we were able to manage a jailbreak and get Liam's authentic self to his wild and sacred place in nature. Though Liam's true self was very comfortable in this sacred place, he would not integrate with Liam in ordinary reality unless Liam agreed to leave the law practice and follow his dream to work in music. Liam was too afraid to change his life, his depression returned and he stopped coming to see me soon after.

## Nourishing Our True Nature

Seen from this perspective, depression is a very twisted form of self-defense or self-rejection. Depression separates us from the light of our highest self, which is why it is almost always experienced as darkness. Our work as humans is to bring forth our own unique, individual truth, no matter how difficult, unpopular or unsavory that might seem in the short run.

If we attempt to avoid or evade our responsibility to support and express our deepest self, the consequences can range from lifelong malaise and lack of fulfillment to chronic depression and suicide.

We are here to bring our own unique, quirky, authentic self into the world. Finding, nourishing, supporting and expressing our true nature is the only path to fulfillment, joy and inner prosperity.

Once a person is able to retrieve their authentic self, commit to do what needs to be done, or make the life changes necessary to support and nourish their true nature, a major internal shift has occurred. This shift brings a sense of wellbeing, personal empowerment, courage, confidence and clarity. On the material plane, opportunities may present themselves for greater professional, creative, or social fulfillment. New friends or romantic partnerships may arrive as we open and resonate from a place of flow and connection with Universal Truth.

There is a spiritual law that the highest good for one person is the highest good for everyone involved. This means that when we raise the bar for ourselves, as we grow in integrity, we are asking others to meet us, to rise to their own authentic self as well.

Water seeks its own level. As we change how we relate to ourselves, the quality of people and circumstances in our lives will change accordingly. With this, we may lose people and situations that no longer serve us. Let them go.

In the words of Marianne Williamson, author of *A Return To Love: Reflections on the Principles of 'A Course In Miracles,'*

> "Your playing small does not serve the world. There is nothing enlightened about shrinking so that other people won't feel insecure around you. We are all meant to shine as children do. We were born to make manifest the glory of God that is within us. It's not just in some of us; it's in everyone. And as we let our own light shine, we unconsciously give other people permission to do the same. As we are liberated from our own fear, our presence automatically liberates others."

## Reclaiming Lost Power

As we saw in the previous chapter, when we work in non-ordinary reality, we have access to ways of managing life energy that are extraordinarily helpful and profoundly healing. The final phase of healing from depression is to restore our systems to full power using an inner journey for *Reclaiming Power Lost Through Depression*.

Depression drains the life energy of a person. When we're depressed, we are rendered incapable of taking constructive action. Like the ancient practice of bloodletting, a twisted attempt at healing, depression weakens the person physically, mentally and emotionally.

When our life energy is returned to us, we have the resources needed to take risks, face our fears, and step into the unknown that all growth and change requires. When we have our life energy back, we can stand in our true power. As light dispels darkness, authentic power dispels depression.

The inner journeys of *Allies & Demons* take us beyond the confines of the conscious mind which is generally limited to the material plane. In the power retrieval process, life energy is literal and not theoretical. Using our active imagination and spiritual help, we are able to reclaim the power we have lost through depression, trauma, stress or illness.

## *Taking The Inner Journeys To Dissolve Depression*

Depression is complex and can be devastating on many levels. For this reason, there are three inner journeys used to heal depression. These inner journeys may want to be done repeatedly as we unravel the layers of depression that imprison the authentic self.

The first inner journey, *Dissolving The Demon Of Depression*, illuminates and resolves the dark energy of the depression directly.

The second process, *Soul Retrieval*, reclaims and heals the authentic self parts lost, rejected, dissociated or cut off by the depression.

The third process is *Reclaiming Power Lost Through Depression*. This journey aims to restore vital life energy lost through depression. Combined in this way, these inner journeys will transform the configuration of depression and reintegrate the life force lost in the depressive experience.

*The three inner journeys to dissolve depression are available in guided audio format at www.reneemckenna.com*

This first process, *Dissolving The Demon Of Depression*, illuminates and resolves the dark energy of the depression directly. This practice is inspired by the ancient Tibetan Buddhist practice known as *Chod*.

## Take a moment to become present...

*Notice how you experience depression in your body. Is it a voice? A sensation? A feeling? Where does the inner critic live in or around your body? Does it have a color? A shape? A density? A temperature?*

*Imagine moving this energy of depression out of your body and personifying it with limbs, a head and face. What size is it? Does it have a gender? What's its emotional state or character? Once the demon of depression is personified, we want to ask it some questions.*

*What does the demon of depression want? What is its purpose? What does it feed on or get out of being with you? What does this demon really need? What is its deepest most vulnerable need or the antidote to it?*

*Imagine that your body dissolves into a nectar or elixir which is exactly the qualities that the demon most deeply needs. What is the quality of the nectar?*

*The nectar moves towards the demon of depression and it can take it in, drink it, receive what it most deeply needs. The nectar might absorb through the covering of its body, pour over it or into it. How does the demon receive what it really needs?*

*There is an unlimited supply of nectar. The demon can drink, absorb or receive to its complete satisfaction. Take all the time it needs to receive. Observe what happens. Does the demon change how it looks or feels? Does it shrink or dissolve completely?*

*Once the demon is completely satisfied, ask if it is an ally in this transformed state or if it needs to move on to the next place for its own evolution. If it needs to move on, the nectar can transport it away, or your guides can escort it safely to the next place.*

If the demon is now an ally, we will ask it the questions that follow. If the demon moved on or dissolved, then ask for an ally to appear. Be open to what comes. When the ally appears, notice its form.

What are the ally's strengths? How will it help you? How will it protect you? What vow or promise does the ally make to you? How can you connect with the ally?

Imagine that the energy of the ally pours into your body. Notice how this energy is transmitted, where it enters your body. Once you are filled with the energy of the ally, bring your awareness into the room and call the ally into ordinary reality. Notice where the ally is in relation to you. How does it feel to have them here?

Write down your experience.

The second process for healing depression, Soul Retrieval, reclaims and heals the authentic self parts cut off, rejected or dissociated by depression.

## *Make yourself comfortable and close your eyes...*

*Take a few deep breaths to relax your body. With each breath, let your awareness drop deeper into your own inner world. Call in the guides and allies you have connected with in previous journeys. See which allies want to be present to bring healing to the authentic part of yourself that was harmed by depression.*

*Notice where this spiritual help is in relation to you. Do the guides and allies create a particular configuration around you? Notice how it feels to have your allies with you in this way.*

*Sense, feel or imagine the part of yourself that needs help. We are seeking the part of you that was cut off, harmed or dissociated by depression. We are here to help this part of yourself so that they don't have to suffer anymore.*

*How old is this part of yourself? What is their setting? What are they doing? How are they feeling?*

*Imagine yourself as you are today, your best adult self with all the experience you've had and all the work you've done. Bring your guides and teachers with you and imagine, sense or feel yourself stepping into the scene with this part of yourself and making yourself known to them. Tell them we are here to help. Tell them the situation they are in happened a long time ago and they don't need to live there anymore. Tell them we're here to bring them into present time so they can heal and be loved and cared for in the way they've always needed. Tell them they don't need to be alone anymore.*

*How is it for this part of yourself to hear this? Do they know who you are? If they don't, tell them that you are their adult self from present time here to help them.*

*How do your guides and teachers feel about this part of you? How does this part of you feel about your guides and teachers? How do you feel about this part of yourself? How does this part feel about you?*

*Is there anything you'd like to do or communicate with this part of yourself right now? What do they need? Can you or your allies provide this for them now?*

*How have you related with this part of yourself in your life? If you've ignored or been unaware of this part of yourself, what effect has this had on them?*

*Ask them if they are willing to leave this place? We want to bring them out of this historic situation which, you can remind them, happened a long time ago. They don't need to live there anymore. We want to bring them into present time. We want to bring them to a safe and sacred space in nature that has only their highest good in mind.*

*Bring this part of you to a beautiful and powerful place in nature right now. It may be a place you've been before or someplace new. Your allies can assist with this if needed.*

*How is it for them to be in this natural place? Assure them that no one can come here without their permission. Anything that happens here is a teaching for their own development and highest good.*

*They can do whatever they want or need to make themselves comfortable - they can rest, explore, receive healing or interact with the elements here.*

*Notice how this part of yourself feels in this place as they become more aware of what's around them. Do they hear or smell anything? Is it day or night? What are the elements in this place? What are the colors and textures? What is the quality of the air?*

*As they become more aware of this place, they might become aware that the spirit of this place is aware of them and is perhaps glad that they have come. How is it for them to open to this deep connection with nature?*

*Is there anything in particular that they feel drawn to or that seems drawn to them? How does it feel for them to be connected in this way in a place of compassion, power, wisdom and support? Assure them that they are safe in this place.*

*Are you willing to care for and love this part of you in the way they've always needed? This is a living relationship and your guides and teachers can help you grow in caring for and supporting this aspect of yourself.*

*Assure this part of yourself that they are in present time now and they need never return to the place of depression. They are in a safe place that has only their healing and evolution as its focus. How is it for them to hear this?*

*Ask them if they want to stay in this place in nature to heal and recover or come and be with you in your life today? It's up to them, but know that you'll have access to them whatever their choice is. The ultimate goal is for them to come and be with you, but they can do that when they're ready.*

*If they do want to be with you, sense, feel or imagine hugging them into your body, breathing them in physically, mentally, emotionally, spiritually, energetically, sexually, socially, relationally, professionally and creatively. You might even feel a filling sensation as you retrieve this aspect of your own soul energy into you.*

*Breathe them in and welcome them home. Imagine their being flowing all the way down the soles of your feet, out to your fingertips and up to the crown of your head, integrating them into every system of your body, adding to your own life force.*

*When this feels complete, ask your guides and teachers if there is anything else that wants to be done or communicated. If this part of yourself wants to stay in this place in nature, that is fine. Assure them that they are safe and supported. You'll be able to be aware of them and check in on them more easily than ever before. Let them know your guides and teachers can stay there with them in their spirit aspect and that they will receive the compassion and healing they need here.*

*Remembering everything fully, come back into your body, mind, emotions and spirit. Take all the time you need and open your eyes when you feel ready.*

*Check in with the part of you that we just connected with. Notice where they are in relation to you in the room. How are they feeling?*

*You might want to take a few moments and write down your experience in a journal or your Allies & Demons Workbook.*

The final process for dissolving depression is *Reclaiming Power Lost Through Depression*. This inner journey restores vital life energy drained away through depressive experience and supports the authentic self in daily life.

# *Make yourself comfortable and close your eyes…*

*Take a few deep breaths and become present. Call in your guides, teachers and any allies you've connected with or any aspects of your own highest self. Viscerally feel where these spiritual allies are in relation to you. Where do you experience them in the room right now?*

*Sense, feel or imagine going to a safe and sacred place in nature where we can do a power retrieval. Your guides and teachers can help you find an appropriate place. Bring them with you.*

*Once you are in this place, call in your guide for power retrieval or ask your allies who can facilitate a power retrieval. Notice where the guides are in relation to you in this place. They may create an energetic configuration around you that will help with power retrieval.*

*If you have experienced power loss from depression, we want to ask this guide or teacher to retrieve the life energy that was lost or drained away. Notice what the guide or teacher does. In the psyche, all time is present time and guides and teachers can gather lost life energy, retrieve it and bring it back to you.*

*You may be able to track them as they go back across space and time to gather that life energy or you may not not. If you are able to track them, notice how they gather up the life energy you've lost. Does your life energy have a form, color or quality? They may go back to the places where life energy was lost or they may gather it in a different way.*

*Your power retrieval guide will return or transmit your life energy back into your body. What is the process they use to return your life energy to your system? In traditional Shamanism, the power is blown into the top of the head. Where does the life energy enter your system? How does this transmission happen?*

*Breathe the energy in. Open to receive this life energy back on all levels; physically, mentally, emotionally, spiritually, energetically. Integrate this energy all the way down to the soles of your feet, out to your fingertips and up to the crown of your head. You might feel a filling sensation or you might not.*

*When that feels complete, ask your guides and teachers if anything wants to be done or communicated to be complete with this for now. When this feels complete, thank the guides for their help and return into your body in ordinary reality. Drink some water and notice how your body feels.*

*Write about your experience.*

# CHAPTER 10

# Facing Our Fear

*Courage is not the absence of fear;
it is the making of action in spite of fear,
the moving out against the resistance engendered by fear
into the unknown and into the future.*

- M. Scott Peck

Outgrowing fear is some of the most important work we do. Fear keeps us stuck in old ways of being and is a destructive, soul-sucking force. Being brave doesn't mean we have no fear. Being brave is doing the scary thing anyway.

The best way to outgrow fear is to practice walking toward what scares us. The good news is that we don't have to go it alone. We may need a lot of help and support along the way. Walking into a dark room by yourself can be frightening. If we bring a friend and a flashlight, it might even be fun. Gathering the resources needed to move through our fears is the purpose of this chapter.

Some schools of thought suggest that there are two opposing energies in the universe - love and fear. All of our feelings, thoughts and actions are motivated by one or the other. Love is the constructive force which propels us forward into greater complexity, joy and engagement with life. Fear constricts us, holds us back, keeps us small, hopeless and helpless.

In surrendering fear, we discover and heal the roots of our own suffering directly. We connect with the unhealed, frightened parts of ourselves and bring them to the transformative power of Spirit in present time. Growing in emotional, social and spiritual maturity is one of the great benefits of this work.

When we bring the frightened, wounded parts of ourselves into present time we become more whole, more grounded, more centered and more able to respond practically to the life decisions and choices that are in front of us. We no longer need to live from a place of reactivity to the past or defend our wounds so that they won't get poked.

It is natural to defend our wounds, like a dog will bite if we pull its broken leg. The problem is that we defend the wounded parts of ourselves so well that they never get to heal.

In this work, it's really important to approach ourselves holistically and to take into account all of the systems that participate in what's happening when we look at fear and anxiety. By the time the body presents a problem, there's probably a lot of other warning signs that have been ignored along the way. Anxiety is a red flag that there is a deeper problem. Discomfort is designed to let us know we are out of balance or being challenged.

Healing anxiety doesn't mean we will never feel fear again. Sometimes fear is important and appropriate. Even so, we can begin this internal parenting process of caring for and nurturing ourselves emotionally, spiritually and even physically in the ways that we've always needed. This brings us to a place of deeper and deeper trust with ourselves and the Universe as we develop the ability to face and walk through fear in a healthy, supported way.

## Faces Of Fear

Where trauma is generally about the past, fear, for the most part, is concern for the future. Most of our fears are rooted in resisting change and a natural distrust of the unknown. Fear can be a very powerful, helpful survival tool. Its purpose is to alert us to circumstances that threaten our wellbeing and to keep us from taking risks.

From ancient times, our bodies and brains are wired for survival. When we were hunters and gatherers, walking into unknown territory presented very real dangers. Our limbic brains still function on instinct and staying with the familiar can keep us safe, but it can also keep us stuck.

Our ancestors were sometimes forced to travel to find food or water. Although it is unlikely we will die of thirst if we don't face our fears, we may die in a different way. We may die on a soul level for lack of fulfillment, meaning or purpose in our lives.

On a physical level, fear sets in motion a cascade of responses in our nervous system that enable us to flee, fight or hide for our own protection. However, fear can far outgrow its intended protective function and become a debilitating demon, often taking on a life of its own.

Fear has many faces: worry, panic, dread, denial, avoidance, procrastination, phobias and timidity. What a list! Anxiety is a fancy word for fear. It might be chronic, episodic or full-blown panic attacks that drive us to the emergency room thinking we're having a heart attack. Or, it just might be a mild sickness to our stomach or nervousness that's always there.

Anxiety might come around specific events or it might come seemingly from nowhere. Anxiety, in my experience, always has a source, and tracing it back to its roots shows us the internal wounds that need to be healed. In fact, anxiety can really be a gift if properly worked with, because it can call us to do deeper healing and personal growth work that we wouldn't do if we didn't have the distress pushing us.

The body, mind and emotions are all inextricably connected. Our intellect likes to create stories to explain our experience and those stories may or may not be accurate. In *Allies & Demons* we go into the body-felt experience of our inner narratives, because the body doesn't lie. The body holds deep information about our fears and anxieties and opens the possibility that we can bring insight, wisdom and healing to places unavailable to the conscious mind alone.

## Evolving Or Devolving

The Life Process is always calling us to grow and evolve. Growth and change often require effort, a move into the unknown or the creation of something completely new. The unknown future may feel alternately scary or exciting depending upon our perspective, our level of trust in the Life Force and our personal sense of adventure.

We're either growing or devolving. Life doesn't have a neutral setting because the very nature of life is change. We're either progressing toward our own highest good or we're actively resisting it. They both take effort. One is constructive, the other is destructive.

The question is, do we want to use our resources to work for our evolutionary good or as resistance that keeps us stuck?

## Procrastination & The Illusion Of Safety

At its core, the function of fear is to help us avoid discomfort or harm. The problem is that the changing nature of existence pulls us into the unknown constantly, which can be inconvenient and even disruptive to our ego-centered plans.

We need to grow to be able to face our fears or we will be in a constant state of avoidance. If we are motivated by love, exploring the unknown can be a fascinating undertaking. If we are ruled by fear, the unknown may be frightening and we will avoid it. We each have our own unique configuration of both love and fear to grapple with.

Putting off, ignoring or evading the things that frighten or challenge us are common tactics to manage our emotions that can actually cause more anxiety than they prevent.

"Procrastination is an emotion regulation problem, not a time management problem," said Dr. Tim Pychyl, professor of psychology at Carleton University in Ottawa. In a 2013 study,[1] Dr. Pychyl found that procrastination is more about being focused on 'the immediate urgency of managing negative moods' than getting on with the task."

Although it would seem like better time planning would solve the procrastination problem, it is only through being willing to face our fears and unresolved emotional baggage that we can live fully in the now and walk through our life challenges.

It is healthy to have concern for our safety. The problem is that we may have trouble discerning between healthy life challenges that call us to grow and realize our potential, and situations that are truly dangerous. Change and progress move us out of our comfort zone. Moving outside of our comfort zone is - uncomfortable.

Our nervous system responds to all fear in a similar way. Learning to tell the difference between the challenging feelings associated with progress and actual harm is really important. If we associate comfort with safety, we may develop a habit of avoiding the natural progression of life.

---

1  Pychyl, Tim. "Procrastination and the Priority of Short-Term Mood Regulation: Consequences for Future Self." WhiteRose.ac.uk. http://eprints.whiterose.ac.uk/91793/1/Compass%20Paper%20revision%20FINAL.pdf

Energy needs to flow. Resisting the Life Force in an attempt to stay safe keeps us stagnant and ultimately disconnected from Universal Flow. Laziness, procrastination, depression, anxiety can all be understood as symptoms of resistance in an attempt to stay safe.

Life is fatal. Although it is wise to stay reasonably safe, we get one chance to live this moment, this day, this particular life. We have free will. We have a choice. Love or fear. Evolution or constriction.

Safety in this context is an illusion, a lie. When we attempt to cheat our life process and avoid the legitimate discomfort of full impact living, we suffer. We live in fear of harm and miss opportunities for joy and fulfillment. We avoid engaging with people, places and things that make us uncomfortable. The avoidance itself becomes a source of pain because on a deeper level we know we are not living our personal best.

Fear is a terrible motivation. When we make decisions based on fear, we are actually choosing death rather than life. When we live from a place of fear we are killing the opportunities for positive change available to us in the many choices we make each day.

Discernment is key. Personal growth, doing new things and taking legitimate risks can produce their own anxiety. Our purpose here is not to live in constant angst in the name of progress. Those of us who suffer chronic anxiety may have grown so used to feeling a constant level of fear that we lose the ability to ascertain what our feelings are trying to tell us. It is not uncommon for an anxious person to stay too long in a bad situation because they believe that they will be anxious no matter what.

For example, my first job out of college was working in the community program department at the local cable TV office. My boss was a jerk. He was condescending and even abusive at times. I wouldn't stay at that job for three days now, but I stayed for a year and a half. I had anxiety every day going to work. We had meetings and memos and interventions about his behavior, but I had such difficulty holding a job up to that time, I promised myself I would stay no matter what.

I thought some of my daily panic was because I had trouble with keeping commitments. After I quit, I felt immediate relief. My feelings had been telling me to get out of there, but I didn't listen. Ironically, that boss got fired for being abusive to the person who took my place about 3 months after I left.

One of the benefits of inner journey work is the development of clarity of mind and emotion. In these journeys, we will cultivate informed decision-making skills based on our feelings and intuition. We will grow our ability to distinguish unhealthy from healthy situations.

## Doing The Scary Thing

I've suffered with chronic anxiety much of my life. My anxiety is always rooted in concern for what will or will not happen in the future. As with most people, this is actually an attempt at self-care and keeping myself safe that doesn't work.

It's important to determine if we are making decisions based on short-term comfort or long-term good. When I was a kid I had a lot of social anxiety and going to school always made me feel nervous and sick to my stomach.

My parents were both pretty avoidant, so they let me stay home from school all the time. I learned that if I said I was feeling sick, I could get out of almost anything. I justified this as telling the truth, because I really did feel sick to my stomach - with nerves. My mother felt that it was loving to let me stay home, because she was offering me comfort and protection by allowing me to avoid things that made me uncomfortable.

Although my mother's aim was to keep me comfortable, the long-term effect was devastating. I learned that discomfort could and should be avoided. I became fearful and insecure. I lacked confidence and skills to handle life problems without collapsing. I didn't develop the inner strength needed to face adversity or learn how to walk through scary or difficult situations.

As a young adult I was unable to hold a job or be emotionally honest in relationships. If it didn't feel good, I wouldn't do it. I quit most jobs within the first month and many relationships didn't last much longer. It took me seven years to graduate college. I was using drugs and alcohol to medicate my fear and self-loathing. It took a lot of intentional work as an adult to gather the skills to just do the scary thing, whatever it was.

This type of "love" is not really loving at all, it is crippling. It keeps us weak and small rather than pushing us to full size. Habitually avoiding difficult life situations creates an illusion of security that ultimately erodes self-esteem. Dodging discomfort also robs us of the opportunities to build healthy resilience and strength of character.

Like vigorous exercise builds strength in our bodies, living a sedentary life makes us weak. Challenging ourselves by facing our fears fosters courage, fortitude, diligence and healthy discipline. We need to be willing to tolerate short-term discomfort and place our long-term good first.

Confronting our fears gives us a sense of achievement and personal power like no other. Each time we do something hard or scary, our anxiety fades and self-confidence grows. Moving out of our comfort zone confirms that we really *do* have the ability to endure difficulties and thrive. We gain a priceless treasure - freedom from debilitating fear. Our greatest challenges provide us with massive opportunities to strengthen, build courage, and evolve.

## Progress Makes Us Happy

Acquiring money, relationships or things does not make people happy. What makes people genuinely happy is progress.

Personal progress is intentionally participating in our own life process. It's about transmuting the energy of resistance into positive, constructive action that supports our own highest good. We may need a lot of help to do the hard or scary things in our lives, but help is available. The two inner journeys for surrendering fear accompanying this chapter will clear old, limiting patterns and connect you with resources to live your potential.

There is an old saying that if we do what we always did, we will get what we always got. It is imperative to move outside of our comfort zone if we want new and different outcomes. Learning to move toward our discomfort by doing what is difficult or frightening is one of the most loving things we can do for ourselves.

As aforementioned, we cannot cheat the evolutionary flow of life without consequence. Though it is common to put short-term comfort over long-term good, the consequences are apathy, avoidance, stagnation and cowardice. Every action creates a reaction. Every inaction has a consequence as well. Conscious or unconscious, inaction is a choice.

M. Scott Peck, in his classic book *The Road Less Traveled*, defines love as "extending oneself for the spiritual growth of another." To call ourselves and others to grow may mean doing things which are difficult, challenging and uncomfortable. We do the hard thing because we want to grow to our full power and potential, not because we are masochists who want to suffer. Love in this context is not about comfort, but about spiritual growth and healthy progress.

Self love requires a willingness to move toward the expression of our highest self. We must extend ourselves for our own spiritual, mental, emotional and physical maturation. This may require all of the courage and personal power we can muster. It may require more than we have alone. We may need to ask for help from others and from The Divine.

## The Delusion Of Independence

When we live deeply and authentically, our fears are replaced by a sense of adventure and fulfillment. The only way out is through. Walking through fear is a practice and, again, we may need a lot of help to move into the unknown. It is not only okay to ask for help, it is imperative. The more we access the human and spiritual help available to us, the more we grow in security and faith in the life and death cycle.

In a full life, we naturally cycle through stages of dependence, independence and interdependence. As humans, we progress from depending on others at birth to get all our needs met, strive for independence as teens or young adults, utilize healthy interdependence as full adults, and then cycle back to dependence as we approach old age and death.

Healthy friendships, romantic or family relationships, community, faith, and work environments are interdependent. There is a give and take which goes both directions and serves everyone more completely than the individuals could manage alone.

Dependence is often frowned upon as weakness in our independence-obsessed culture. But none of us is truly independent. We are part of a web of life, interdependent with and depending on many living and non-living things for our survival. We breathe air created by plants. We eat other life forms, even if we are vegan. The structures we inhabit and the clothing we cover ourselves with are all part of our interdependence with the world of form.

Even if we sit in a room alone with a computer each day, we are interacting with the computer and sitting on a chair in a building, all of which were created by other humans. We have to breathe, eat and go to the bathroom. In these ways we are dependent and interdependent in almost all areas of our lives.

Interdependence is mutually beneficial dependence between two or more entities. We may take our physical dependence on food, clothing and shelter for granted. Yet the idea of being interdependent for our emotional, social and spiritual needs can be a foreign or even negative concept. We may see any form of dependence as a weakness or have an ego that puffs itself up with the delusion of independence as a source of pride.

Alternately, we may fear that others will let us down or expect something in return if we ask for help. We may feel that our way of doing things is better and not trust others to be responsible, efficient or effective. We may have been taught that it is shameful to need or ask for help. We may believe that we should intuitively know how to manage life situations even if we have no experience with them.

It can feel vulnerable to be honest about our needs, deficits and difficulties. However, exposing our authentic needs is the only way they will ever be met.

## Receiving

We need to grow in the ability to tell the truth about our own needs and vulnerabilities. Being honest about our shortcomings opens us to receive from others and from God. When we are open to receive, we step more fully into the flow of life and grace rises to meet us.

In the words of Brené Brown, author of *Daring Greatly: How The Courage To Be Vulnerable Transforms The Way We Live, Love, Parent and Lead*, "Vulnerability sounds like truth and feels like courage. Truth and courage aren't always comfortable, but they are never weakness."

Many people believe that if they ask for help they are a burden or a drain. Certainly there are those in perpetual need who do drain and suck the life energy of others. Asking others to do for us what we need to develop the capacity to do for ourselves is avoidance and a form of faulty dependence.

There is an old Diné proverb which states, "Give a man a fish and you feed him for a day. Teach a man to fish and you feed him for a lifetime." We need to be willing to learn how to fish for our own highest good. With practice and self honesty, we learn when to ask for help in healthy ways.

When we ask for help and open to receive it, we are asking others to give to us. Most people are much more comfortable giving than receiving, but if no one is the receiver then there is no place to genuinely give. When we are willing to receive and learn from others, we actually help them by providing an opportunity for them to experience giving.

Authentic giving and receiving is a feedback loop that serves both the giver and the receiver. In this way, receiving is actually a service to those from whom we ask for help because there is nothing more fulfilling in life than to genuinely help another human being. This is the spiritual law of service; *all good service serves the server.*

From a spiritual perspective, we are each a unique expression of Divine Energy. Our feelings of disconnection and isolation are central to our suffering as humans, but from the perspective of Ultimate Reality, we are all connected.

Opening to authentic giving and receiving is like plugging our laptop into the charger. We connect with a source of unlimited potential and access the world wide web of life. We experience ourselves as part of a great whole. We feel loved and loving. We step into the flow of life and access the support and guidance of Creative Reality.

However, we need to be willing to step outside of our ego-system and into the great stream of the unknown and unknowable. Fear wants us to stay "safe" in the familiarity of the shoreline. As the actor

Will Smith says, "God placed all the best things in life on the other side of fear."

The inner journeys for surrendering fear will provide the help and power we need to make the gentle step, stride or leap into the proverbial water of our own evolution, whatever our personal style may be.

## Caring For Our Authentic Needs

There is a level of existential angst that goes with modern life. All feelings have an origin in our body/mind/spirit complex. In fact, it could be understood that the chronic, low level anxiety many feel is actually a healthy response to the unhealthy aspects of Western culture.

Many of the norms of modern life are pretty harmful. Most of us are overworked, sleep-deprived, over-caffeinated, sedentary, screen-obsessed and isolated. Surprise! We're anxious. No wonder the use of psych meds has skyrocketed over the past fifty years.

What is considered culturally normal or acceptable, can actually be quite toxic to the individual. Yet we frequently try to jam our round peg into the square hole of the over-culture and pay the price of our peace of mind and the health of our bodies.

## Isabel's Anxiety

For example, Isabel was a plump, jovial, human resources manager, who had suffered from anxiety since childhood. Though she did well at work and had lots of friends, her chronic angst and constant self-criticism sapped the joy out of her life.

The gap between Isabel's outer life and her inner life was extreme. She was a very bright and friendly young woman who seemed to move easily in social situations, but inwardly never felt good enough.

Isabel's mother was an alcoholic. As a child, her father had worked long hours and watched a lot of TV when he was home. She learned at an early age to pay close attention to minute details of the house and mother's behavior to know if mom was drinking or not. Sometimes her mom was sugar sweet, sometimes raging and violent. As a result, Isabel became an expert at reading people and situations.

In our work together, it became clear that Isabel was extremely perceptive and highly sensitive to the emotions of others. Not only was she hyper-aware of her environment and the people in it, she actually took the negative energy of other people into her body in an unconscious effort to keep the peace. In fact, some of her anxiety was an attempt at processing all the external energy she took on in daily life.

Isabel's mother had tried to stop drinking many times over the years and Isabel was deeply affected by her mother's continuously unpredictable behavior. Using the *Transforming The Demon Of Fear* journey accompanying this chapter, we were able to clear and process a lot of the negative energy Isabel had taken on from her relationships and general life. Her natural sensitivity became apparent and she worked on her inner self-parenting and self love.

Over time Isabel realized that watching the news, violent TV and reading social media were like a minefield for her. She unknowingly absorbed much of the fear and negativity put out through these media channels into her own system.

As she became aware of how bad she felt after engaging in mainstream media, Isabel decided to follow her own best interest and cut back dramatically on screen time in general. Though at times it was a social challenge, she made a healthy choice to support her own wellbeing.

We did a lot of work creating healthy boundaries to manage the energy of others and the world at large. Through the profound tools of power retrieval and exchange, she was able to safely extract and expel the negativity she had taken on over the years. This cleared a lot of internal space and brought a shift in her anxiety level.

Isabel decided to continue her personal work by attending meetings of Adult Children of Alcoholics and Al Anon.

## Make Friends With Our Feelings

Anxiety can also be a sign that there are unfelt emotions that need to be felt and expressed. Making room for our deeper feelings is an important practice to keep us emotionally balanced and in tune with our inner truth. Modern life is filled with busyness and we have more opportunity for distraction than any generation before us.

Relief from some anxiety can be as simple as taking a few minutes to sit quietly each day and get in touch with our feelings on a body level. Opening to our emotions connects us with our felt experience of life. Feelings provide information about who we are, what we need, want, and how we relate to others.

Emotions also provide a digestive process for our daily experience. If we hold in our feelings, the effects can be similar to holding in going to the bathroom. It makes us sick. We become emotionally and energetically constipated. Our physical digestion allows us to absorb vital nutrients from food and excrete what is not helpful. Our emotions allow us to process and receive information and nourishment from our interactions and release that which doesn't serve us.

If we put off, ignore or deny our feelings, a backlog can develop. It is common for people to fear connecting with their emotions because they are afraid that once the floodgates are open, the feelings will overwhelm them or never stop. This creates a layer of fear and emotional avoidance on top of the original emotion. This layering can be a set up for low level fear or chronic anxiety. These are misguided attempts at emotional regulation which sap our life energy.

The solution is to create a safe internal space where we can make friends with our feelings without judgment. Feelings are the color, flavor and texture of life. They connect us with ourselves and with others directly and vulnerably. Learning to manage our internal emotions in a healthy way is important for our relationship with ourselves and with others.

## Psychological Torture

My son came home one day and said he learned about psychological torture in his psychology class. He said, "You know that the research says fear of pain is worse than the pain itself." I didn't need a scientific study to tell me that. What his insight did clarify is that I had been performing psychological torture on myself for decades in a twisted attempt at keeping myself safe.

The underlying idea is that if I can predict what will happen, I can prepare myself for it. If I'm prepared for what's going to happen, the thinking goes, I will feel less powerless and have some illusion of control.

The problem is that the future doesn't really exist. My future projections were negative fantasies about bad outcomes. These negative projections cause fear in the present about things that have not and might never actually happen.

From this point of view, anxiety can be seen as a form of self-torture. The intended purpose, of course, is control and self-protection. It's related to the belief that thinking or worrying about things is the same as doing something about them.

Bad news: thinking about things generally does little to change them and may even reinforce choices that actually create the very things we fear.

For some of us, anxiety is produced by projecting a series of worst case scenarios on to possible future outcomes and practicing living through them. That's the self-torture model. Procrastination, as just mentioned, attempts to manage anxiety by putting off or denying the feared or difficult actions. Other people may keep themselves compulsively busy to avoid feeling anything at all. Still others may manage anxiety by planning and organizing every aspect of life, creating a false idea of control and finding some safety in knowing what to expect.

Certainly it can be helpful to take time to plan, organize and carefully consider our decisions. However, once a plan or a decision is made, we need to let go of the outcome. Letting go of outcome requires a certain amount of trust in The Universe. For many, there is a direct correlation between the amount of anxiety we have and the level of safety we feel in the world at large.

## Hypervigilance

Hypervigilance can take many forms, but it usually means that the sufferer is acutely aware of what is happening and pays strict attention to even the smallest changes as a flag that danger may be approaching. Isabel became hypervigilant due to her childhood experience.

Hypervigilance can be physical, mental, emotional and energetic. This is a different way to understand the motives driving someone who is controlling or compulsive.

For example, we might obsessively check our bank balance, need to weigh ourselves every day or track our likes on social media. The numbers associated with these areas of our lives may become intertwined in an unhealthy way with feelings of self-worth and safety. If a pound is gained or lost, if a check clears or a post goes un-liked then we might feel secure or insecure as the numbers come in.

Others might be hyper-aware of the actions and reactions of others, constantly looking for approval, disapproval, love or rejection in every interaction. Some need to control their physical environment to manage emotions, running the extremes from compulsive cleanliness to hoarding. Often these techniques to manage feelings are learned in childhood, either directly or in polar response to early experiences.

## Epigenetics

There is a lot of evidence that life experience can affect our genetic coding in subtle but profound ways. Called epigenetics, there is a growing body of evidence that suggests experience is passed down just like our eye and hair color.

"Neuroscientists at Emory University found that genetic markers, thought to be wiped clean before birth, can transmit a single traumatic experience across generations, leaving behind traces in the behavior and anatomy of future offspring.

In one experiment, researchers taught male mice to fear the smell of cherry blossoms by associating the scent with mild foot shocks. Two weeks later, they bred with females. The resulting pups were raised to adulthood having never been exposed to the smell. Yet when the critters caught a whiff of it for the first time, they suddenly became anxious and fearful. They were even born with more cherry-blossom-detecting neurons in their noses and more brain space devoted to cherry blossom smelling.

The memory transmission extended out another generation when these male mice bred, and similar results were found."[2]

For those of us who feel we may have inherited the fears and dysfunctions of our ancestors, there is much that can be done. On a soul level there are no victims, only volunteers. There is nothing in our psyche without our agreement, even though this agreement might

---

2   Parental olfactory experience influences behavior and neural structure in subsequent generations Brian G Dias & Kerry J Ressler. published online Sunday in the journal Nature Neuroscience. Reported in the Washington Post By Meeri Kim December 7, 2013 Health & Science. "Study finds that fear can travel quickly through generations of mice DNA"

be unconscious. Once we become conscious, we have the power to make profound changes.

Building on our work with ancestors from Chapter 4, we can actively release the patterns of our tribe and create new healthier configurations to pass on to future generations. On a spiritual level, these inherited patterns can be viewed as sacred vows or even as family curses. These vows or curses are like energetic contracts or agreements that we make on a soul level.

The great news about soul level agreements is that we can renegotiate them at any time to reflect our personal growth. We can update our ancestral contracts just like we can change jobs, move homes or shift the way that we relate to people over time.

## The Twisted Vow

Robert had a lot of anxiety about money. Although he had a college degree, he worked mostly boring entry level jobs that barely paid him enough to live on. He felt doomed to be unhappy and unfulfilled.

Through inner journey work we discovered a twisted vow or belief that ran through his family line. The vow went something like, "life is a struggle and the son should not surpass his father."

Robert's father had died alone in a crummy studio apartment a few years back. Robert had not seen him in the months leading up to his death and felt a lot of guilt about being a bad son.

In looking back at family history, it was clear that Robert's father had a similar experience with Robert's grandfather. Guilt and obligation to the dead parent gave energy to the vow, creating unconscious agreements through the male lineage to struggle and not be more successful than previous generations. It was essentially a vow of poverty, failure and disappointment, inherited like blue eyes or curly hair. The good news is unlike physical traits, epigenetic experience can be rewired.

Once we clarified the family belief, Robert worked on rewriting a new spiritual contract around work and money. He connected with his ancestral line and released the old vow.

A few months later, Robert started a teacher certification program and in a few years got a job as a teacher. He had always dreamed of teaching, but couldn't pursue it while his father was alive because teaching wasn't a job his father would have approved of.

Robert was freed of his father's disapproval and began living a new, more authentic contract stating that he could be happy and fulfilled in his work. He released the obligation to match the experience of his ancestors and walked through his own fear of success and failure which drove his anxiety.

In this way, it is my belief that epigenetics can be used to our advantage, in that we are always adapting to change on the deepest levels. Why can't that change be positive or constructive? If mice can be trained for a genetic predisposition to fear, why can't we train for a tendency toward hope, courage, love and creativity?

Rather than being helpless victims of our parents' experiences, we have endless opportunities to create new ways of being for ourselves and those who will follow us.

## Releasing Fear

Surrendering to the natural flow of life is the only sane path. Fear, generally rooted in an attempt to stay safe and avoid discomfort, is a boogeyman that resists this natural flow. Through the inner journeys that follow, we will transcend and transform our fears. As a result, valuable life energy becomes available for us to use in constructive and positive ways for the benefit of ourselves and others.

In *Allies & Demons* anxiety can be healed. I can't tell you it is going to be healed by Tuesday, but I can tell you from my own personal experience, having suffered with both anxiety and depression, chronic and long-term, that they can be healed. The important thing to know is that our presenting symptoms are always pointing to a deeper issue, perhaps a range of deeper issues. When we heal the underlying problem then the symptoms resolve themselves.

For many of us, this is the beginning of a lifetime practice for recognizing and releasing fears as they arise. In the journeys that follow, we will connect with Spirit in present time. We will ground ourselves in compassionate energy and seek to heal the core wounds that generate our fears and anxieties.

## *Taking The Inner Journeys To Surrender Fear*

There are three inner journeys to surrender fear. The first is *Transforming The Demon Of Fear* to release the energetic patterns of worry, fear and anxiety. The second journey, *Soul Retrieval*, heals and cares for the vulnerable parts of the self that may be driving the fearful patterns. The final process is an inner journey for *Reclaiming Power Lost Through Fear*, to recover life energy lost through our fearful, anxious experiences. These inner journeys may want to be done repeatedly as we release our fears and grow in emotional vulnerability and maturity.

*Alternately, you can listen to the guided audio for these three inner journeys at www.reneemckenna.com.*

This first process for *Transforming the Demon Of Fear* releases and dissolves the energetic pattern of worry, fear or anxiety directly using the power of compassion.

## *Take a moment to become present...*

Notice where fear, worry or anxiety live in your body. We are going to be curious and use our active imagination to clarify. If the fear had a color, what color would it be? Does it have a shape? A density? A temperature? It doesn't need to make any sense.

Imagine moving the fear energy out of your body and personifying it with limbs, a head and face. What size is it? Does it have a gender? What's its emotional state or character? Once the demon of fear is personified, we want to ask it some questions.

What does the demon of fear want? What is its purpose? What does it feed on or get out of being with you? What does this demon really need? What is its deepest most vulnerable need or the antidote to it?

Now, imagine that your body dissolves into a nectar or elixir which has exactly the qualities that the demon most deeply needs. What are the qualities of the nectar?

The nectar moves toward the demon of fear. This demon can take it in, drink it, receive what it most deeply needs. The nectar might absorb through the covering of its body, pour over it or into the top of its head. How does the demon receive what it really needs?

There is an unlimited supply of nectar. The demon can drink, absorb or receive to its complete satisfaction. Be patient and just let the demon take all the time it needs to receive. Observe what happens as the demon integrates and is infused with exactly what it really needs. Does the demon change how it looks or feels? Does it shrink, fade away or dissolve?

Once the demon is completely satisfied, ask if it is an ally in this transformed state or if it needs to move on to the next place for its own *evolution. If it needs to move on, the nectar can transport it away, or your guides can escort it safely away.*

*If the demon is now an ally, we will ask it the questions that follow. If the demon moved on or dissolved, then ask for an ally to appear. Be open to what comes. When the ally appears, notice its form.*

*What are the ally's strengths? How will it help you? How will it protect you? What vow or promise does the ally make to you? How can you connect with the ally in daily life?*

*Now, imagine that the energy of the ally pours into your body. Notice how this energy is transmitted, where it enters your body. Once you are filled with the energy of the ally, bring your awareness into the room and call the ally into ordinary reality. Notice where the ally is in relation to you. How does it feel to have them here?*

*Write down your experience.*

This second process for surrendering fear, *Soul Retrieval*, reclaims and heals the authentic self parts rejected, dissociated or cut off by fear and anxiety. Chronic anxiety can damage many aspects of the self. For this reason, you may want to repeat this Soul Retrieval process multiple times to restore yourself to health and wholeness.

## *Make yourself comfortable and close your eyes…*

*Take a few deep breaths to relax your body. With each breath let your awareness drop deeper into your own inner world. Call in the guides and allies you have connected with in previous journeys. See which allies want to be present to bring healing to the authentic part of yourself that was harmed or lost because of fear.*

*Notice where this spiritual help is in relation to you. Do the guides and allies create a particular configuration around you? Notice how it feels to have your allies with you in this way.*

*Sense, feel or imagine the part of yourself that needs help. We are seeking the part of you that dissociated, or was cut off or wounded by fear. This may be a fearful part of you, or it might not. We are here to help this part of yourself so that they don't have to suffer anymore.*

*How old is this part of yourself? What is their setting? What are they doing? How are they feeling?*

*Imagine yourself as you are today, your best adult self with all the experience you've had and all the work you've done. Bring your guides and teachers with you and imagine, sense or feel yourself stepping into the scene with this part of yourself and making yourself known to them. Tell them we are here to help. Tell them the situation they are in happened a long time ago and they don't need to live there anymore. Tell them we're here to bring them into present time so they can heal and be loved and cared for in the way they've always needed. Tell them they don't need to be alone anymore.*

*How is it for this part of yourself to hear this? Do they know who you are? If they don't, tell them that you are their adult self from present time here to help them.*

*How do your guides and teachers feel about this part of you? How does this part of you feel about your guides and teachers? How do you feel about this part of yourself? How does this part feel about you?*

*Is there anything you'd like to do or communicate with this part of yourself right now? What do they need? Can you or your allies provide this for them now?*

*How have you related with this part of yourself in your life? If you've ignored or been unaware of this part of yourself, what effect has this had on them?*

*Ask them if they are willing to leave this place? We want to bring them out of this historic situation which, you can remind them, happened a long time ago. They don't need to live there anymore. We want to bring them into present time. We want to bring them to a powerful, safe and sacred space in nature that has only their highest good in mind.*

*Bring this part of you to a beautiful place in nature right now. It may be a place you've been before or someplace new. Your allies can assist with this if needed.*

*How is it for them to be in this natural place? Assure them that no one can come here without their permission. Anything that happens here is a teaching for their own development and highest good.*

*They can do whatever they want or need to make themselves comfortable - they can rest, explore, receive healing or interact with the elements here.*

*Notice how this part of yourself feels in this place as they become more aware of what's around them. Do they hear or smell anything? Is it day or night? What are the elements in this place? What are the colors and textures? What is the quality of the air?*

*As they become more aware of this place, they might become aware that the spirit of this place is aware of them and is perhaps glad that* they have come. How is it for them to open to this deep connection with nature?

Is there anything in particular that they feel drawn to or that seems drawn to them? How does it feel for them to be connected in this way in a place of compassion, power, wisdom and support? Assure them that they are safe in this place.

Are you willing to care for and love this part of you in the way they've always needed? This is a living relationship and your guides and teachers can help you grow in caring for and supporting this aspect of yourself.

Assure this part of yourself that they are in present time now and they need never return to the place of depression. They are in a safe place that has only their healing and evolution as its focus. How is it for them to hear this?

Ask them if they want to stay in this place in nature to heal and recover or come and be with you in your life today. It's up to them, but know that you'll have access to them whatever their choice is. The ultimate goal is for them to come and be with you, but they can do that when they're ready.

If they do want to be with you, sense, feel or imagine hugging them into your body, breathing them in physically, mentally, emotionally, spiritually, energetically, sexually, socially, relationally, professionally and creatively. You might even feel a filling sensation as you retrieve this aspect of your own soul energy into you.

Breathe them in and welcome them home. Imagine their being flowing all the way down the soles of your feet, out to your fingertips and up to the crown of your head, integrating them into every system of your body, adding to your own life force.

When this feels complete, ask your guides and teachers if there is anything else that wants to be done or communicated. If this part of yourself wants to stay in this place in nature, that is fine. Assure them that they are safe and supported. You'll be able to be aware of them *and check in on them more easily than ever before. Let this part of yourself know that your guides and teachers can stay there with them in their spirit aspect and they will receive the compassion and healing they need here.*

*Remembering everything fully, come back into your body, mind, emotions and spirit. Take all the time you need and open your eyes when you feel ready.*

*Check in with the part of you that we just connected with. Notice where they are in relation to you in the room. How are they feeling?*

*Take a few moments and write down your experience.*

The final phase of healing from fear is to restore our systems to full power using the *Inner Journey To Reclaim Power Lost To Fear & Anxiety*. This journey helps us to restore and reclaim the power we have lost through fear.

## *Take a few deep breaths and become present...*

*Call in your guides, teachers and any allies you've connected with or any aspects of your own highest self. Viscerally feel where these spiritual allies are in relation to you. Where do you experience them in the room right now?*

*Sense, feel or imagine going to a safe and sacred place in nature where we can do a power retrieval. Your guides and teachers can help you find an appropriate place. Bring them with you.*

*Once you are in this place, call in your guide for power retrieval or ask your allies, "Who can facilitate a power retrieval?" Notice where the guides are in relation to you in this place. They may create an energetic configuration around you that will help with power retrieval.*

*If you have experienced power loss from fear, worry or anxiety, we want to ask this guide or teacher to retrieve the life energy that was lost or drained away. Notice what the guide or teacher does. In the psyche, all time is present time and guides and teachers can gather lost life energy, retrieve it and bring it back to you.*

*You may be able to track them as they go back across space and time to gather that life energy or you may not not. If you are able to track them, notice how they gather up the life energy you've lost. Does your life energy have a form, color or quality? They may go back to the places where life energy was lost or they may gather it in a different way.*

*Your power retrieval guide will return or transmit your life energy back into your body. What is the process they use to return your life energy to your system? In traditional Shamanism, the power is blown into the top of the head. Where does the life energy enter your system? How does this transmission happen?*

*Breathe the energy in. Open to receive this life energy back on all levels; physically, mentally, emotionally, spiritually, energetically. Integrate this energy all the way down to the soles of your feet, out to your fingertips and up to the crown of your head. You might feel a filling sensation or you might not.*

*When that feels complete, ask your guides and teachers if anything wants to be done or communicated to be complete with this for now. When this feels complete, thank the guides for their help and return into your body in ordinary reality. Drink some water and notice how your body feels.*

*Write about your experience.*

# Going Forward:
# Spiritual Practice In Daily Life

*Be not lax in celebrating. Be not lazy in the festive service of God.
Be ablaze with enthusiasm. Let us be an alive,
burning offering before the altar of God.*

- Hildegard of Bingen

Spiritual practice is to the soul as exercise is to the body. It is both grounding and nourishing to find a practice that works for us and a rhythm that is sustainable. Spiritual practice is a specific activity or time dedicated to connecting with your own highest self or the God of your understanding. For some people this looks like prayer and meditation. Some garden or walk in nature. For others, a temple, mosque, church or synagogue is the place to contemplate Spirit through communal prayer and sermons. Some connect using body-centered practices like yoga, running and martial arts. Others find Higher Consciousness through music, art, dance or poetry.

Living on the California coast, I know many whose spiritual practice is surfing and being immersed in the immensity of the ocean. Working with crystals, pulling tarot cards, reading runes and studying astrology can be portals to Divinity as well. Doing community service work, feeding the homeless and donating to charity can also be spiritual practices.

Anything that expands our consciousness, connects us with a larger reality or provides principles for living a life of integrity can be a spiritual practice. Practice is the key word.

To practice is to do something over and over for the joy of doing it or to improve. The thing about practice is that we never achieve mastery and stay there. Just as we need to move and challenge our bodies to maintain strength and flexibility, we need to exercise our spiritual muscles to grow and maintain connection.

One never masters spirituality. There is always more to learn. Practice not only teaches us new things, it keeps us in good form and maintains what we have already gained.

Itzhak Perlman, arguably the premier violinist in the world, still practices the violin three hours every day. Golden State Warriors point guard Steph Curry, one of the greatest basketball shooters of all time, makes 500 shots per day in the summer and makes 200 to 350 shots per day during the season. People get good at things when they do them a lot.

## Daily? Really?

Honestly, I find it daunting to do anything on a daily basis aside from eating, sleeping and walking my dogs. Over the years I have had many teachers suggest daily practice. Although I have had periods of time when I did journey, meditate or do yoga daily, these have been the exception rather than the rule.

There are those who say you only benefit from 20 minutes of silent sitting meditation; that doing less is ineffective. I find this not only untrue but closed-minded and discouraging.

One mindful breath is better than no mindfulness at all. Sitting quietly for one minute is better than never getting centered. Walking to the store occasionally is more exercise than none. In this light, I encourage you to find a rhythm of spiritual or personal growth practice that works for you. Trust your own process.

I find small, doable, achievable goals are much more effective than lofty, ambitious ones. We move through life one day at a time, one step at a time. Discovering the sweet spot of sustainable action is confidence building, joy producing and life affirming. Easy does it, but do it!

## Creating Sacred Space

Creating a spiritual space or place in our home can make regular practice easier and more enjoyable. Having a comfortable, peaceful and beautiful place to take the inner journeys of *Allies & Demons* can be helpful in a few ways.

Humans are creatures of habit and developing the habit of dedicating time for our own evolution can be very rewarding. Part of developing a habit is to do the same thing in a similar way over and over. With each repetition the behavior becomes easier and more familiar.

Creating a sacred space can be as simple as having a nice place to sit or lie down where we will be undisturbed. It might be a favorite chair, our bed or kitchen table.

Creating a space that reflects our own spirituality can be fun and empowering. We might make a place on the dresser or fireplace mantle to put photos, quotes, fresh flowers or other objects that feel significant or inspiring. We might even get a special table or chair especially for this purpose. Decorating or decluttering a space makes room for Spirit in an intentional way. Marie Kondo, the organizing guru, calls this "making room for God."

Sacred space can be as simple as a single candle or as beautiful, complex or elaborate as one can imagine. When we consciously create sacred space, we are creating a ritual.

Ritual is the act of calling Spirit into the material world. Whether we create a complicated altar with artwork and relics or a simple, quiet sitting space for our practice, we are inviting the Divine into our homes and into our lives in a direct way. Many find that making sacred space brings an element of peace and depth that enhances their entire home.

## Journeying In Groups

Doing inner journeys with a friend or in a group setting offers power and support that isn't available when working alone. Walking the path of personal growth work with others can be a community building, life-changing experience.

As we share our experience, strength and hope with each other, our vision of ourselves and our shared humanity both expands and heals us. The group experience is nearly always greater than the sum of its individual members. God works through people and lives most fully in a group of seekers with a shared vision. With this is mind, readers may be inspired to take the inner journeys of *Allies & Demons* in community, either with partners, friends or small groups.

Some find it helpful to have a therapist or spiritual advisor to meet with on a regular basis while working the *Allies & Demons* program. There is a list of resources at the back of this book of helpful organizations and additional reading.

*If you would like to attend a workshop or book a remote or in-person session of Allies & Demons work, email info@reneemckenna.com or visit my website at www.reneemckenna.com.*

AWAKEN THE WISDOM OF YOUR AUTHENTIC SELF

# ALLIES & DEMONS

## WORKBOOK

WORKING WITH SPIRIT FOR POWER AND HEALING

RENEE LAVALLEE MCKENNA, MA, CCH

# *Allies & Demons Workbook*

Many practitioners prefer to journey on their own. There are advantages of convenience, comfort and time flexibility that make working solo easy and attractive. Simply find a quiet, comfortable place and take the inner journeys accompanying each chapter or listen to the guided audio journeys available on my website. Let Spirit guide you as It most certainly will.

You may want to use the *Allies & Demons Workbook* created for individuals and groups to simplify and enhance your experience of this work. This helpful workbook provides deepening questions, space for art and journaling, and additional processes for healing and transformation not included in this text.

You can purchase this supportive workbook through www.reneemckenna.com.

# Resources

The following is a list of resources, organizations and reading materials to help you on your personal growth path. You may want to delve deeper into one or more of the affiliated organizations, or simply study the materials.

**Renee LaVallee McKenna, MA, CCH**
*Allies & Demons* combines the ancient healing and wisdom traditions of Shamanism and Buddhist psychology with the best of Western psychology to create a powerful medicine for the mind, body and spirit. Beyond healing our mental and emotional suffering, *Allies & Demons* works on a soul level to empower and activate your authentic self, the source of true joy and fulfillment. For information on workshops, events, podcasts or to book a remote or in-person session please visit:
info@reneemckenna.com
https://www.reneemckenna.com
https://www.facebook.com/Allies-Demons-104327894315339/
https://www.instagram.com/alliesanddemons/
https://twitter.com/alliesanddemons
https://www.linkedin.com/company/allies-demons

**Tara Mandala**
Tara Mandala offers a complete path of meditation practice and study from beginning instructions in meditation, mindfulness, and compassion to deep retreat in the tradition of Vajrayana Buddhism. https://www.taramandala.org/

### The Foundation Of The Sacred Stream
Classes and training in Depth Hypnosis, Applied Shamanism, Buddhist Studies, and Energy Medicine. Founded by Dr. Isa Gucciardi, Ph.D. and located in Berkeley, CA.
https://sacredstream.org/

### Lifespan Integration
Lifespan Integration is a gentle, body-based therapeutic method which heals without re-traumatizing.
https://lifespanintegration.com/

### Clairvision
The Clairvision School provides meditation training at the highest level, emphasizing the superiority of first-hand knowledge over belief. http://www.clairvision.org/

### The International Pathwork Foundation
This organization disseminates and sustains the legacy of Eva Pierrakos, author of the Pathwork Lectures, a series of 258 channeled lectures delivered from 1957 to 1979. These lectures emphasize the need for honest self-examination on the path of self-realization and provide a range of profound concepts and tools to help us undertake the process of self-transformation.
https://pathwork.org/

### The Foundation For Shamanic Studies
Based on years of founder Michael Harner's research and experimentation, core Shamanism consists of the universal, near-universal, and common features of Shamanism, together with journeys to other worlds.
https://Shamanism.org/

### Family Systems Therapy (FST)
As a clinical treatment, FST has been rated effective for improving phobia, panic, and generalized anxiety disorders, physical health conditions, personal resilience and depression.
https://www.selfleadership.org/

### Hakomi Institute
The Hakomi Method is a mindfulness, somatic and experience-based approach to change. This method is used both as a psychotherapeutic process as well as in educational settings to facilitate self-exploration and personal growth.
https://hakomiinstitute.com/

**Twelve Step Recovery**

**Alcoholics Anonymous** is an international fellowship of men and women who have found a solution to their problems with alcohol.
https://www.aa.org/

**Al-Anon** is a worldwide fellowship that offers a program of recovery for the families and friends of alcoholics, whether or not the alcoholic recognizes the existence of a drinking problem or seeks help.
https://al-anon.org/

**Narcotics Anonymous** has a group atmosphere that provides help from peers and offers an ongoing support network for addicts who wish to pursue and maintain a drug-free lifestyle.
https://www.na.org/

**Overeaters Anonymous** says that no matter what your problem with food - compulsive overeating, under-eating, food addiction, anorexia, bulimia, binge eating, or over exercising - they have a solution.
https://oa.org/

**Sex & Love Addicts Anonymous** is a program for anyone who suffers from an addictive compulsion to engage in or avoid sex, love, or emotional attachment.
https://slaafws.org/

**Sex Addicts Anonymous** is a Twelve-Step program of recovery from sex addiction.
https://saa-recovery.org/

**Debtors Anonymous** is a twelve-step program for people who want to stop incurring unsecured debt.
https://debtorsanonymous.org/

**Underearners Anonymous** is a twelve-step program for men and women who have come together to overcome what they call underearning and under being.
https://www.underearnersanonymous.org/

**Codependents Anonymous** is a twelve-step program for people who share a common desire to develop functional and healthy relationships.
http://coda.org/

**Workaholics Anonymous** is a twelve-step program for people identifying themselves as "powerless over compulsive work, worry, or activity." Workaholics include overworkers and those who suffer from unmanageable procrastination or work aversion.
http://www.workaholics-anonymous.org/

**Recovering Couples Anonymous** is a twelve-step program for couples committed to restoring healthy communication, caring, and greater intimacy to their coupleships.
https://recovering-couples.org

# Suggested Reading List

*Feeding Your Demons: Ancient Wisdom for Resolving Inner Conflict* by Tsultrim Allione

*Codependent No More: How to Stop Controlling Others and Start Caring for Yourself* by Melody Beattie

*Daring Greatly: How the Courage to Be Vulnerable Transforms the Way We Live, Love, Parent, and Lead* by Brené Brown

*The Hero's Journey* by Joseph Campbell

*The 7 Habits of Highly Successful People* by Stephen R. Covey

*Living Buddha, Living Christ* by Thich Nhat Hanh

*Shamanic Journeying: A Beginner's Guide* by Sandra Ingerman

*A Path with Heart* by Jack Kornfield

*Anatomy of the Spirit: The Seven Stages of Power and Healing* by Caroline Myss

*Lifespan Integration: Connecting Ego States through Time* by Peggy Pace

*The Road Less Traveled: A New Psychology of Love, Traditional Values, and Spiritual Growth* by M. Scott Peck

*Women Who Run With The Wolves: Myths and Stories of the Wild Woman Archetype* by Clarissa Pinkola Estés, Ph.D.

*Entities: Parasites of the Body of Energy* by Samuel Sagan, M.D.

*Regression Past-Life Therapy for Here & Now Freedom* by Samuel Sagan, M.D.

*The Undefended Self: Living the Pathwork* by Susan Thesenga

*The Power of Now: A Guide to Spiritual Enlightenment* by Eckhart Tolle

*A Return to Love: Reflections on the Principles of "A Course in Miracles"* by Marianne Williamson

Made in the USA
Monee, IL
01 February 2020